Essential Music Theory
Levels 7-8

Mark Sarnecki

Elementary Music Theory © 2023 by San Marco Publications. All rights reserved.

All right reserved. No part of this book may be reproduced in any form or by electronic or mechanical means including Information storage and retrieval systems without permission in writing from the author.

ISNB: 9781896499390

Contents

Lesson 1: **Scale Review**	1
Lesson 2: **The Chromatic Scale**	12
Lesson 3: **The Whole Tone Scale**	18
Lesson 4: **The Octatonic Scale**	20
Lesson 5: **The Pentatonic Scale**	22
Lesson 6: **The Blues Scale**	24
Lesson 7: **Clefs**	27
Lesson 8: **Modes**	32
Lesson 9: **Intervals**	39
Lesson 10: **Rhythm and Meter**	49
Lesson 11: **Triads**	73
Lesson 12: **Seventh Chords**	89
Lesson 13: **Cadences**	99
Lesson 14: **Transposition**	124
Lesson 15: **Score Types**	137
Lesson 16: **Melody Writing**	150
Lesson 17: **History**	162
Lesson 18: **Music Analysis**	188
Music Terms and Signs	202
Exams	208

This volume covers Levels 7 and 8 of Essential Music Theory. The abbreviations for these levels are ❼ and ❽ and they appear in the left margin of the page. These symbols indicate the level of the material being covered. The number ❼ refers to Level 7; the number ❽ refers to Level 8. Level 7 material is required for Level 8.

1
Scale Review

The Circle of Fifths

Figure 1.1 is the circle of 5ths with major and minor keys. The ***circle of 5ths*** is a chart organizing all of the keys into a system that is used to relate them to one another. At the top, is the key of C major, which has no sharps or flats in its key signature. Each stop on the circle moving clockwise from C is a key with one more sharp than the previous key. Each stop moving down counter-clockwise from C is a key with one more flat than the last key.

Figure 1.1

Key Signatures

Figure 1.2 shows the placement of sharps and flats on the grand staff.

Figure 1.2

Technical Names for Scale Degrees.

Every scale degree has a technical name. Here are the names for each scale degree.

$\hat{1}$ Tonic
$\hat{2}$ Supertonic
$\hat{3}$ Mediant
$\hat{4}$ Subdominant
$\hat{5}$ Dominant
$\hat{6}$ Submediant
$\hat{7}$ Leading tone

1. 1. Write the following scales ascending and descending in whole notes Use a key signature for each.

G flat major

B major

F sharp major

Minor Scale Review

There are three types of minor scales:

1. **natural minor**: uses the same key signature as its relative major.
2. **harmonic minor**: is the natural minor with $\hat{7}$ raised a half step.
3. **melodic minor**: is the natural minor with $\hat{6}$ and $\hat{7}$ raised a half step ascending, and lowered a half step descending.

Figure 1.3 show all three versions of the D minor scale.

Figure 1.3

D natural minor

D harmonic minor

D melodic minor

The Subtonic and the Leading Tone

There are two technical names for scale degree $\hat{7}$. The names depend on the scale and the relationship of $\hat{7}$ to the tonic.

When scale degree $\hat{7}$ occurs in the major scale it is one half step away from the tonic. In this case, it leads to the tonic and is called the **leading tone**.

When scale degree $\hat{7}$ is raised in the harmonic and ascending melodic minor scales it is one half step away from the tonic it is called the **leading tone**.

When scale degree $\hat{7}$ is not raised in the natural minor and the descending melodic minor scales, it is a whole step away from the tonic and is called the **subtonic**.

1. Write the following scales ascending and descending in whole notes. Use a key signature for each.

D flat major

The enharmonic tonic minor of D flat major, harmonic form

The relative minor of D flat major, melodic form

E flat minor, harmonic form

The parallel major of E flat minor

F sharp minor, natural form

The relative major of F sharp minor

C minor, melodic form

Finding The Key of a Composition

The key signature is the first level of organization in a piece of music. The key determines what pitches will occur in a piece. Key signatures are directly related to major and minor scales. A lot of the music we study today adheres to this system of major and minor, and knowing key signatures is an easy way to understand the key of a piece of music.

Study Figure 1.4. This melody has a key signature of three flats. This means that it is in the key of E♭ major or it's relative minor, C minor. The melody starts and ends on E♭ and does not contain any accidentals. Therefore it is in the key of E♭ major. It is important to note that this melody starts and ends on the tonic, but not all melodies will do this.

Figure 1.4

The melody in Figure 1.5 has a key signature of three flats indicating E♭ major or C minor. It also contains B♮. B♮ is not a note in the key of E♭ major. This is a clear indication of the key of C minor. B♮ is raised $\hat{7}$ of C minor. The melody also starts and ends on C, the tonic of C minor.

Figure 1.5

When determining the key of a melody consider the following:

1. The key signature and the two keys, major and minor, that it represents.
2. Accidentals. An accidental may be raised $\hat{7}$ or $\hat{6}$ of a minor key.
3. The beginning and ending notes. Melodies often start and end on the tonic of the key.
4. Look for chords that may be outlined in the melody. For example, a melody in G major may outline the G major triad G - B - D.

❼ Sometimes the key of a melody will not be as clearly defined as the examples we have just seen.
❽ Study the melody in Figure 1.6. Two flats in the key signature indicate B♭ major or G minor. There are no accidentals in this melody. If it were in G minor, there should be raised $\hat{7}$ (F♯). However, this melody does not contain an F so we don't know if it would be raised. The first note is G, and the last note is G. The first measure outlines the notes of the G minor triad and the melody itself seems to center around the note G. In fact, G occurs five times. The key of this melody is G minor.

Figure 1.6

Minor key melodies may contain notes from the natural, harmonic, and melodic minor scales. The key signature of the melody in Figure 1.7 indicates F major or D minor. There are no accidentals. D minor may have raised $\hat{7}$ (C♯), but the one C in this melody is natural. The pick up is A followed by D on the first strong beat. The final note is D. The second measure outlines the notes of the D minor triad. The C♮ is in a descending line that indicates the melodic form of the D minor scale. A D minor melody may have B♭, B♮, C♯ or C♮ depending on how it is written, and the harmony it implies. This melody is in D minor.

Figure 1.7

Sometimes melodies contain accidentals that are used purely for chromatic decoration. These accidentals add color and variety to the music but are not part of the actual key. The melody in Figure 1.8 has the key signature of one sharp. This indicates G major or E minor. There is a C♯ in measure 2. In measure three, C is natural, and there are no D♯s anywhere in the melody. It starts and ends on G. Therefore, the C♯ is a chromatic decoration of the D on either side of it, or a more complex chord, and the melody is in the key of G major.

Figure 1.8

1. Name the keys of the following melodies.

Vite

key:

Largo

key:

Allegretto

key:

Moderato

key:

Andante

key:

Allegro

key:

Alla marcia

key:

Presto

key:

2. Name the keys of the following musical excerpts.

Anton Diabelli
Allegretto

key:

Carl Czerny
Study

key:

Arcangelo Corelli
Sarabande

key:

Johannes Brahms
Waltz Op. 39. No. 3

key:

Finding a Key Without a Key Signature

You may have to determine the key of a composition that uses accidentals instead of a key signature. Follow these steps :

Determine if the melody uses flats or sharps. Figure 1.9 uses flats. List the flats in order and check them off as you find them in the music. This melody has two flats, B♭ and E♭. This indicates the keys of B♭ major or G minor. There are no other accidentals. G minor may have F♯, but F is not sharp here. The melody begins on B♭ and is in the key of B♭ major. It is written using a key signature in Figure 1.10.

Figure 1.9

Hector Berlioz
Symphony Fantastique, IV

B̶ E̶ A D G C F

Figure 1.10

Hector Berlioz
Symphony Fantastique, IV

The melody in Figure 1.11 uses sharps. Write the sharps in order and check them off as you find them in the music. There are three sharps. The keys of A major and F♯ minor have three sharps. However, there is no E♯ indicating raised $\hat{7}$ in F♯ minor. The music starts and ends on A. This is in the key of A major. This melody is written using a key signature in Figure 1.12.

Figure 1.11

Ludwig van Beethoven
Sonata no. 3 for Cello and Piano

F̶ C̶ G̶ D A E B

Figure 1.12

Ludwig van Beethoven
Sonata no. 3 for Cello and Piano

Figure 1.13 contains flats. However, B♭ is missing from the order of flats in this melody. You cannot have a key signature with E♭, A♭, and no B♭. We can assume that the B♮ is an accidental. This melody is in the key of C minor which has three flats and raised $\hat{7}$ (B♮). Figure 1.14 is the melody written using a key signature. B natural is needed for raised $\hat{7}$.

Figure 1.13

Antonio Vivaldi
Concerto

B E̶ A̶ D G C F

Figure 1.14

Antonio Vivaldi
Concerto

1. Name the keys of the following melodies. Rewrite them using a key signature and any necessary accidentals.

Joseph Haydn
Quartet, Op. 76

Key: _____

Joseph Haydn
Symphony No. 99

Key: _____

Johann Sebastian Bach
English Suite 6, Courante

Key: _____

Frederic Chopin
Nocturne Op. 72. No. 1

Key: _____

Frederic Chopin
Sonata for Cello and Piano

Key: _____

2

The Chromatic Scale

❼❽ The *chromatic scale* is made up of half steps. It has twelve pitches. Since it contains the same intervals throughout it is considered a *symmetric scale.* If you play a chromatic scale starting on C, you play every note ascending until you get to the next C, and then do the same descending. The notation of the chromatic scale may vary, but the simplest way to write a chromatic scale is to write sharps ascending and flats descending.

Figure 2.1 is an ascending chromatic scale starting on C. Sharps are used as the scale ascends. Half steps occur between E - F and B - C. When you write a chromatic scale, notate these white key half steps using natural notes. For example, don't write F as E♯.

Figure 2.1

Figure 2.2 shows the C chromatic scale descending. Flats are used for the descending form of this scale. Flats are commonly used when notes move downward chromatically, and sharps are used for chromatic passages that ascend. The white key half steps C - B and F - E are notated as natural notes.

Figure 2.2

❼ When writing the chromatic scale ascending and descending and it is a good idea to use a bar line
❽ at the top of the scale before moving down. This cancels all the previous accidentals. See Figure 2.3.

- When writing any chromatic scale do not use the same letter name more than twice.
- Never change the name of the tonic enharmonically. For example, if the scale starts on C♯ it must end on C♯, not on D♭.

Figure 2.3

When a chromatic scale starts on a flat, use sharps as soon as possible as you ascend. The A♭ chromatic scale in Figure 2.4 cannot change to sharps until C♯ because no letter name can be used more than twice. Notice that it does not end on G♯ at the top. It must end on the same note that it starts, in this case, A♭.

Figure 2.4

1. Write the following chromatic scales ascending and descending.

Chromatic scale on F

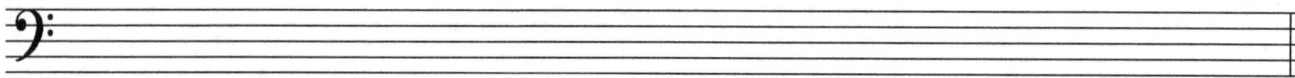

Chromatic scale on D♭

7
8

Chromatic scale on E

Chromatic scale on G#

Chromatic scale on A

Chromatic scale on G♭

Chromatic scale on B

Chromatic scale on F#

❼ The notation of a chromatic scale may vary if it is written in a specific key. In this case, the key sig-
❽ nature will be the guide to the accidentals used in the chromatic scale.

For example, if a sharp-based key signature is used, sharps are used for the chromatic notes in the scale. The D chromatic scale in Figure 2.5 uses the key signature of D major. Since this is a key signature using sharps, the chromatic scale uses sharps. It is important to be aware of the key signature and adjust any notes accordingly.

Figure 2.5

The chromatic scale in the key of B♭ uses the key signature of B♭ major. This is a flat-based key signature. The added chromatic scale notes are not part of that key. However, since the key signature uses flats, the chromatic scale uses flats ascending and descending.

Figure 2.6 is the B♭ flat chromatic scale using a key signature. When writing this scale, begin with the key signature and the starting note. Since flats are used in the key of B♭ major, move each note up and down chromatically using flats. It is helpful to think of the keyboard when writing chromatic scales. Never use a letter name more than twice.

Figure 2.6

1. Write the following chromatic scales using key signatures for each.

F chromatic scale

A chromatic scale

E♭ chromatic scale

B chromatic scale

A♭ chromatic scale

F♯ chromatic scale

❼ 2. Circle any chromatic passages that occur in the following musical excerpts.
❽

Henry Purcell
Dido and Aeneas, Didos Lament

Ludwig van Beethoven
Sonata Op. 2, No. 2, IV

3
The Whole Tone Scale

The *whole tone scale* is a symmetric scale. It is constructed entirely of whole steps. This is a six-note scale. There are two different whole tone scales. One starting on C, and one starting on C♯. Starting on any other note will create the same pitches as those starting on C or C♯.

Figure 3.1 shows these whole tone scales. When writing this scale:

- Start and end on the same note. Do not change the tonic enharmonically.
- Use six different letter names.
- Do not mix sharps and flats. Use one or the other.

The whole tone scale is often used in movie music during dream sequences since it has a unique dreamy sound. Composers in the twentieth century, most notably Claude Debussy, used this scale in their compositions.

Figure 3.1

❼ 1. Add accidentals to the following to create whole tone scales.
❽

2. Write whole tone scales ascending and descending on the following notes.

on G♭

on B

on E♭

4
The Octatonic Scale

The *octatonic* or *diminished scale*, as it is sometimes known, has eight different notes ("octa" means eight). The octatonic scale is a symmetrical scale. It is built using alternating whole and half steps. There are two forms of this scale. One starts with a whole step followed by a half step. The other starts with a half step followed by a whole step.

Figure 4.1 shows the two versions of this scale starting on C. Composers, like Stravinsky, Scriabin, and Bartok used this scale. It is common in jazz music as well.

Figure 4.1

Whole - Half Octatonic

Half - Whole Octatonic

There are only three octatonic scales. The octatonic scales built on C, C♯, and D are the only ones that use unique sets of notes. If you start an octatonic scale on any other note you will get scales with notes identical to those found on C, C♯, or D.

It is important not to change the first note of this scale enharmonically. For example, if it starts on C♯, it must end on C♯.

1. Add accidentals to create octatonic scales. Do not change the first note of each scale.

2. Write the following octatonic scales ascending and descending.

E octatonic, starting with a whole step

C# octatonic, starting with a half step

A♭ octatonic, starting with a whole step

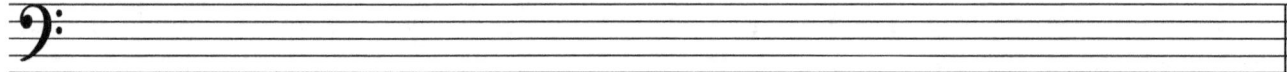

G octatonic, starting with a half step

©San Marco Publications 2023   The Chromatic Scale

5

Pentatonic Scales

Pentatonic scales are five note scales. The prefix "penta" is from the Greek meaning five, and tonic means tones or notes. Pentatonic scales are used in folk, rock, jazz and church music. There are two types of pentatonic scales: major and minor.

The Major Pentatonic Scale

The *major pentatonic scale* is a five-note scale that is related to the major scale. In the major pentatonic scale two notes are omitted from the major scale: $\hat{4}$ and $\hat{7}$.

The C major pentatonic scale is: C D E G A C. This is shown in Figure 5.1.

Figure 5.1

1. Write the following major pentatonic scales ascending only.

D major pentatonic

F major pentatonic

E♭ major pentatonic

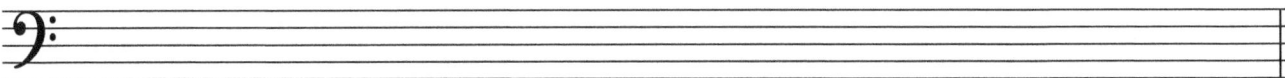

The Minor Pentatonic Scale

The *minor pentatonic scale* is another five note scale. This scale is a natural minor scale with two notes removed. To form a minor pentatonic scale, remove $\hat{2}$ and $\hat{6}$ from the natural minor scale. The A minor pentatonic scale is: A C D E G A. This scale is shown in Figure 5.2.

Figure 5.2

1. Write the following minor pentatonic scales ascending only.

G minor pentatonic

E minor pentatonic

C minor pentatonic

B minor pentatonic

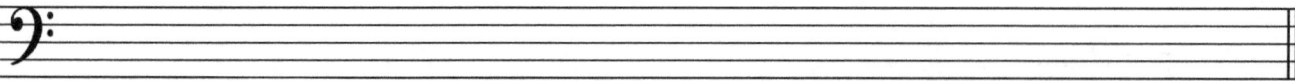

6
The Blues Scale

The ***blues scale*** can be created by altering notes of the major scale. The altered notes are called "blue" notes. These notes originated with African slaves brought to America. A blue note was created by bending the pitch of a note when singing.

The blues scale is the major scale with $\hat{3}$, $\hat{5}$ and $\hat{7}$ lowered a half step. $\hat{5}$ occurs twice, once lowered and once in its original form. Scale degrees $\hat{2}$ and $\hat{6}$ are omitted.

Figure 6.1 contains the C blues scale.

Figure 6.1

1. Add accidentals to the following to create blues scales.

🎧 2. Write the following blues scales ascending.

🎧 E blues

A♭ blues

G blues

F blues

🎧 3. Write the following blues scales descending.

🎧 A blues

C blues

B blues

D blues

The Chromatic Scale

4. Identify the following scales as: major, natural minor, harmonic minor, melodic minor, chromatic, whole tone, octatonic, major pentatonic, minor pentatonic, or blues.

7
Clefs

Why do we use different clefs? Wouldn't it be easier just to use one clef? To understand why we need different clefs look at Figure 7.1 and 7.2. Figure 7.1 is a melody in the treble clef. If we wanted to write this melody in the bass clef as shown in Figure 7.2, we would have to use a lot of ledger line notes, and they can be hard to read. Different clefs allow the notes to stay on and around the staff and make the music easier to read.

Figure 7.1

Figure 7.2

C Clefs

A ***C clef*** establishes the location of the note C on the staff. This is middle C on the piano. Wherever the little notch in the center of the clef occurs is where middle C is located. Figure 7.3 is a C clef with middle C on the third line.

Figure 7.3

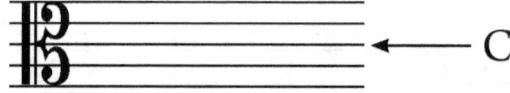

❽ The C clef is different than other clefs because it is a ***movable clef***. Depending on which line the clef indicates, the name is different. The C clef can be placed on various lines of the staff.

Figure 7.4 shows four different C clefs. We will study the alto and tenor clef.

Figure 7.4

The Alto and Tenor Clef

The ***alto clef*** is used by the viola and the ***tenor clef*** is used by the 'cello, trombone, and bassoon. Other C clefs are not used today. Figure 7.5 shows the alto and tenor staves with notes.

Figure 7.5

❽ 1. Name the following notes.

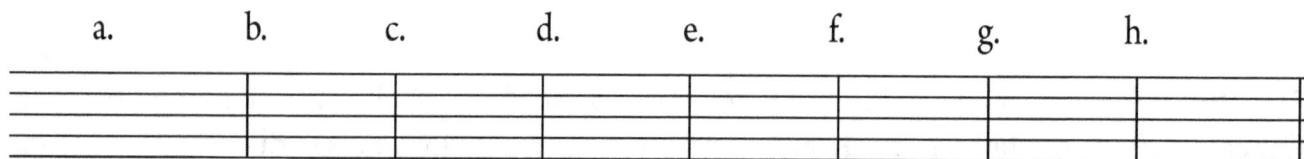

2. Draw an alto clef and write the following notes.

       a. E on a line   e. middle C
       b. B in a space   f. D on a line
       c. D in a space   g. E in a space
       d. F on a line   h. A in a space

a.   b.   c.   d.   e.   f.   g.   h.

3. Draw a tenor clef and write the following notes.

       a. middle C   e. G in a space
       b. D in a space   f. D on a line
       c. E in a space   g. B in a space
       d. F on a line   h. A on a line

a.   b.   c.   d.   e.   f.   g.   h.

❽ 4. Rewrite the following passage using the alto clef.

Wolfgang Amadeus Mozart
Cosi fan tutte

5. Rewrite the following passage using the tenor clef.

Gabriel Faure
Elegie, Op. 24

Key Signatures in the Alto and Tenor Clef

Figure 7.6 illustrates the placement of sharps and flats on the alto and tenor staff.

Figure 7.6

1. Write the following key signatures in the alto clef.

   D major   G minor   F minor   A major   E♭ major   B major

   C♯ major   B♭ minor   E minor   C♭ major   G♭ major   F♯ major

2. Write the following key signatures in the tenor clef.

   G major   C minor   F♯ minor   E major   D♭ major   D major

   B major   B minor   C♯ minor   C♯ major   C♭ major   E♭ minor

8
Modes

A *mode* is a type of scale. Modes are also called "church modes" because they were originally used by the Catholic church in Medieval times. Modes were used to compose the melodies of Gregorian chant and remained in use throughout the Middle Ages. With the rise of the major and minor tonal system in the Baroque era, modes were rarely used in the Baroque, Classical, and the majority of the Romantic eras. They were revived by the Impressionist composers and are used most frequently today by rock and jazz players in improvisation and composition.

There are seven modal scales. Each major scale can be approached from seven different angles with one mode starting from each note of the scale. We will examine each mode using the key of C.

Ionian

The **Ionian mode** is the same as the **major scale**. All the white keys on the piano from C to C. It has the same patterns of whole and half steps as the major scale. It is used in all Western music from classical to rap. Figure 8.1 is the C Ionian mode.

Figure 8.1

Dorian

The **Dorian mode** begins on the 2nd degree of the major scale. Using the scale of C it goes from D to D. **This is the same as a natural minor scale with raised $\hat{6}$.** This mode is used in rock, jazz, blues and fusion music. Figure 8.2 is the D Dorian mode.

Figure 8.2

⑧ Phrygian

The ***Phrygian mode*** begins on the 3rd degree of the major scale. Using the scale of C, it goes from E to E. **This is the same as a natural minor with lowered $\hat{2}$.** This mode has a Spanish sound and is used in Flamenco and fusion music. Figure 8.3 is the E Phrygian mode.

Figure 8.3

Lydian

The ***Lydian mode*** begins on the 4th degree of the major scale. Using the scale of C, it goes from F to F. **This is the same as a major scale with raised $\hat{4}$.** This mode is used in country, rock, jazz, blues and fusion music. Figure 8.4 is the F Lydian mode.

Figure 8.4

Mixolydian

The ***Mixolydian mode*** begins on the 5th degree of the major scale. Using the scale of C, it goes from G to G. **This is the same as a major scale with lowered $\hat{7}$.** This mode is used in rockabilly, country, rock, and blues music. Figure 8.5 is the G Mixolydian mode.

Figure 8.5

Aeolian

The ***Aeolian mode*** begins on the 6th degree of the major scale. **This mode is also the natural minor scale.** Using the scale of C, it goes from A to A. It is used in most music including pop, country, rock, jazz, blues, classical, hip-hop, rap, etc. Figure 8.6 is the A Aeolian mode.

Figure 8.6

⑧ Locrian

The *Locrian mode* begins on the 7th degree of the major scale. Using the scale of C, it goes from B to B. **This is the same as a natural minor scale with lowered $\hat{2}$ and lowered $\hat{5}$.** It is the least commonly used mode but can be found in some jazz and fusion music. Figure 8.7 is the B Locrian mode.

Figure 8.7

Writing Modes

When writing modes, it is helpful know their order. Here is a saying to help you remember the order of modes: *I Don't Punch Like Muhammad A-Li.*

Let's say we are asked to write the B♭ dorian mode.

1. First, the dorian mode starts on $\hat{2}$ of a major scale.
2. Determine what major scale has B♭ as scale degree $\hat{2}$, (A♭ major).
3. Write the mode from B♭ to B♭ using the key signature of A♭ major (4 flats).
4. You're done! See Figure 8.8.

Figure 8.8

To write the A mixolydian mode.

1. The mixolydian mode starts on $\hat{5}$ of a major scale.
2. Determine what major scale has A as scale degree $\hat{5}$, (D major).
3. Write the mode from A to A using the 2 sharps of D major (F♯ and C♯).
4. Modes use accidentals. See Figure 8.9.

Figure 8.9

D major

A mixolydian

⑧ Another Way to Look at Modes

There is an important aspect to understand about modes. Even though modes look like they are derived from notes within a major scale, you should learn and know the modes as their own entities. For example, the G Mixolydian mode (G-A-B-C-D-E-F-G) looks a lot like the traditional G major scale (G-A-B-C-D-E-F#-G). The only difference is the G Mixolydian mode contains an F♮, and the G major scale contains an F#. You could look at this mode as an altered type of major scale. In other words, a major scale with a lowered $\hat{7}$.

Looking at modes as comparable to most major or minor scales can make them easier to understand. Here is a list of the modes and how they relate to major and minor scales.

1. **Ionian** is the major scale
2. **Dorian** is a natural minor scale with a raised $\hat{6}$
3. **Phrygian** is a natural minor scale with a lowered $\hat{2}$
4. **Lydian** is a major scale with a raised $\hat{4}$
5. **Mixolydian** is a major scale with a lowered $\hat{7}$
6. **Aeolian** is the natural minor scale
7. **Locrian** is a natural minor scale with lowered $\hat{2}$ and $\hat{5}$

It can help to remember the modes using the above method. In this way, you can learn them as distinct scales and write and identify them easily. For example, if you wanted to write the A Dorian mode, you would just write an A natural minor scale with a raised $\hat{6}$ (F#).

Figure 8.10

A dorian

1. Write the following modes ascending using accidentals instead of a key signature.

C lydian

G phrygian

E mixolydian

C dorian

D aeolian

F locrian

E♭ lydian

F♯ mixolydian

Identifying Modes

It is fairly simple to identify a mode. One way is to know the order of the modes, and on what degree of the major scale they occur. To identify the mode in Figure 8.11:

1. Collect the accidentals to determine the major scale. Here, there are three sharps indicating the scale of A major.
2. What is the starting note of the mode? Here it is D. D is the fourth note of the A major scale.
3. The Lydian mode begins on the fourth degree of the major scale. That makes this the D Lydian mode.

Figure 8.11

Modes can also be identified easily if you know the relationship between modes and the major and minor scales stated earlier. The Lydian mode is the major scale with a raised $\hat{4}$. Figure 8.11 is a D major scale with a G♯. This quickly identifies it as the D Lydian mode.

1. Identify the following modes.

9
Intervals

Review

The interval is a unit of measurement in music. It represents the distance between two pitches. Study the intervals in Figure 9.1. In order for an interval to be major or perfect the top note must be a member of the bottom notes scale.

In a), B is the third note of the G major scale, making it a major 3rd. If the top note is lowered one half step, (B♭) it becomes minor. If the top note is lowered a whole step, (B♭♭) it becomes diminished.

In b), when the bottom note is raised one half step (G♯) it becomes minor. When the bottom note is raised a whole step it becomes diminished.

In c) and d), the major interval becomes augmented by raising the top note one half step (B♯) or lowering the bottom note one half step (G♭).

Perfect intervals (1, 4, 5, 8) never become minor. In e), lowering the top one half step makes the 4th diminished. Raising the top note a half step makes it augmented.

Figure 9.1

The unison requires special consideration. Since there is no distance between the notes of a unison, it cannot be made smaller. Unisons can never be diminished intervals. If any note of a unison is altered, the notes become further away from each other, and it becomes augmented.
Study Figure 9.2.

Figure 9.2

This chart shows the relationship between intervals. The arrow indicates the movement of the top note one half step.

diminished ← minor ← **major** → augmented

diminshed ← **perfect** → augmented

Solving Intervals

Use the following steps to determine an interval:

1. Count the notes from the bottom up to determine the interval number. Always start by counting the bottom note as 1. In Figure 9.3 A to F is a 6th. A-B-C-D-E-F is 1-2-3-4-5-6.
2. Determine, by the number, if the interval should be major or perfect. A 6th would be major interval.
3. Decide if the top note is a member of the bottom notes major scale. Here, F♮ is not a member of the A major scale since A major has an F♯. It has been lowered one half step making this interval a minor 6th.

Intervals are always solved using the lowest note as the key note. This is true even if the lowest note comes after the highest note in a melodic interval. The lowest note in the second interval in Figure 9.3 comes after the highest note but the interval is still a minor 6th.

Figure 9.3

min 6   min 6

1. Name the following intervals.

Writing an Interval Below a Given Note

You may be asked to write an interval below a given note. Let's say you have to write a major 6th below C. Figure 9.4. illustrates the following steps.

1. Write the note that is a 6th below C.
2. A 6th below C is E.
3. Check the interval quality. In this case E to C is a minor 6th. We need a major 6th, so you have to lower the E to E♭ in order to get a major 6th. Note: You cannot change the given note (C).

Figure 9.4

1. Write the following intervals below the given notes.

Inverting Intervals

Any interval can be inverted or flipped upside down. Figure 9.5 shows the perfect 4th G - C inverted in the second measure. When you invert a perfect 4th it becomes a perfect 5th. Here, C -G.

Figure 9.5

When an interval is inverted the sum of the original and the inverted interval equals nine. Using the intervals in Figure 9.5, G -C is a perfect 4th. When it is inverted it becomes C-G, a perfect 5th. When you add 4 and 5 you get 9. Study the interval inversions in Figure 9.6. They all add up to 9.

Figure 9.6

Except for perfect intervals the interval quality changes when you invert them. Here is what happens to the interval qualities when you invert them:

- major becomes minor
- minor becomes major
- diminished becomes augmented
- augmented becomes diminshed
- perfect stays perfect

The augmented octave is a special case when inverting. An augmented octave is larger than an octave and when it is inverted the numbers do not add up to 9. Figure 9.7 shows the inversion of the augmented octave. An aug 8 becomes a dim 8 when inverted. However, since a dim 8 is smaller than an octave, it becomes and aug 1 when inverted.

Figure 9.7

1. Name the following intervals. In the staff below, invert them and rename them.

2. Name the following intervals.

3. Write the following intervals above the given notes. Invert them and name the inversions.

4. Name the following melodic intervals.

Frederic Chopin
Ballade, Op 23, No. 1

Enharmonic Change

If you change a note enharmonically, you change its name but not its pitch. Figure 9.8 shows enharmonic notes. Each measure contains two notes of the same pitch, but with a different name.

Figure 9.8

The intervals in each measure of Figure 9.9 sound exactly the same, but are named differently. The top note in example a) is changed enharmonically from B♭ to A♯, and the bottom note in example b) is changed enharmonically from A♭ to G♯. Even though the pitch does not change, the interval number and quality changes.

Figure 9.9

1. Name the following intervals. In the second measure change the lower note enharmonically and rename the interval. The first one is done for you.

dim 5   aug 4

2. Name the following intervals. In the second measure change the upper note enharmonically and rename the interval.

Compound Intervals

Intervals larger than an octave are called *compound intervals*.

Figure 9.10

The easiest way to solve a compound interval is to bring the top note down an octave. This puts the interval in its simple form, which is an octave or less. The compound interval will be the same as the simple interval plus 7. The quality of the interval remains the same from simple to compound form.

Figure 9.11

The compound interval can be inverted by moving the upper note down an octave and the lower note up an octave. This reverses the notes. See Figure 9.12. The size of the compound interval and its inversion will add up to 16.

Figure 9.12

1. Name the following intervals. Invert and rename them.

2. Write the following intervals above the given notes.

❽ 3. Name the intervals under the brackets.

1._____ 2._____ 3._____ 4._____ 5._____

4. Name the intervals indicated by the lines.

1._____ 2._____ 3._____ 4._____ 5._____

6._____ 7._____

10
Rhythm and Meter

Dotted Notes

A dot placed just to the right of a note or rest increases its value by half. A whole note receives 4 beats. A dot beside it, adds half of that (2 beats), for a total of 6 beats. 4 + 2 = 6. Figure 10.1 contains dotted notes in quarter time. Dotted rests have the same values.

Figure 10.1

Dotted Whole Note 6 beats	𝅝·	=	𝅝	+	𝅗𝅥
Dotted Half Note 3 beats	𝅗𝅥·	=	𝅗𝅥	+	♩
Dotted Quarter Note 1 ½ beats	♩·	=	♩	+	♪
Dotted Eighth Note ¾ beat	♪·	=	♪	+	♬

7/8 Double Dotted Notes

An additional dot may be added to an already dotted note or rest. The second dot increases the duration of the note or rest by half the value of the first dot. Figure 10.2 shows double dotted notes and equivalent values. Double dotted rests have the same values.

Figure 10.2

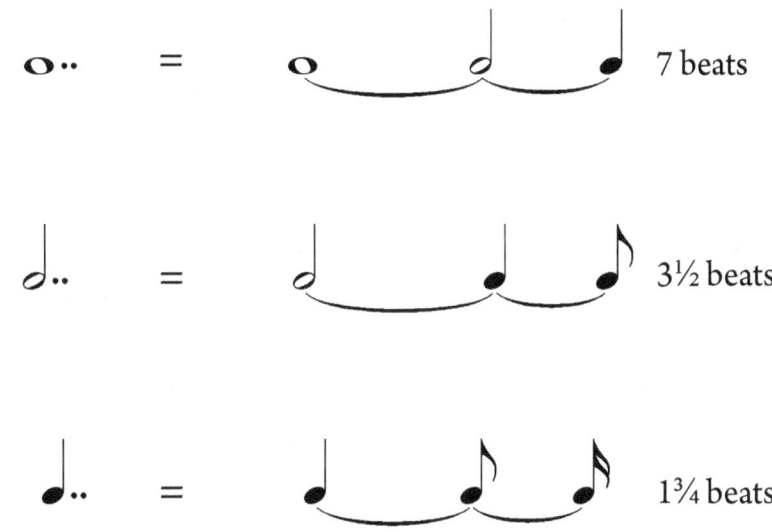

A double dotted note is usually followed by whatever note finishes the measure or the beat. Figure 10.3 illustrates this. Notice the double dotted eighth note in measure 2 which is worth ⅞ of a beat. This is usually joined with a thirty-second note to make one complete beat.

Figure 10.3

1. Complete the following:

   a. 1 eighth note equals _____ sixteenth notes.
   b. 1 dotted half note equals _____ quarter notes.
   c. 1 dotted eighth note equals _____ sixteenth notes.
   d. 1 dotted whole note equals _____ half notes.
   e. 1 dotted whole note equals _____ quarter notes.
   f. 1 double dotted quarter note equals _____ sixteenth notes.
   a. 1 double dotted whole note equals _____ quarter notes.
   b. 1 double dotted half note equals _____ eighth notes.

2. Write a single note which is equal to the the value of the following.

3. Write a single rest which is equal to the the value of the following.

Rhythm and Meter

Simple and Compound Time

Simple time signatures divide the beat into two equal parts. Compound time signatures divide the beat into three equal parts.

Rhythm and Meter

1. Add bar lines according to the time signatures.

❼ 2. Add time signatures at the beginning of each line.
❽

Irregular Divisions of the Beat

A *tuplet* is the general name for a group of notes that do not follow the normal rules of counting. *Triplets, duplets, quadruplets, quintuplets, sextuplets,* and *septuplets* are all tuplets.

For review, a *triplet* is a group of three notes played in the time of two notes of the same value. Triplets generally occur in simple time Figure 10.4.

Figure 10.4

A *duplet* is a group of two notes played in the time of three notes of the same value. Duplets occur in compound time representing a group of three pulses or one beat Figure 10.5.

Figure 10.5

❼ 1. Add bar lines to the following according to the time signatures.
❽

❼ In simple time the beat may be divided into irregular groups of three, five, six or seven. A group of
❽ 5, 6, or 7 notes is played in the time of a group of 4 of the same kind in simple time.

Figure 10.6

In compound time the beat may be divided into irregular groups of two, four, five, or seven. In compound time the main beat is a dotted note. Each group represents one beat (three pulses). Some of the groups look the same in simple and compound time. To determine the beat in the melody with irregular groupings look at the time signature and the other beats in the bar.

Figure 10.7

❼ Many composers used irregular groupings in their work. Figure 10.8 is an example of irregular groups
❽ in a composition by Tchaikowsky. Here, each group represents one beat in simple time.

Figure 10.8

Peter Il'yich Tchaikowsky

❼ 1. Add bar lines to the following excerpts which begin on the first beat of the bar.
❽

Stephen Heller
Prelude, Op. 119, No. 30

Peter Il'yich Tchaikowsky
Nutcracker Suite (Danse Arabe)

Joseph Haydn
Variations Hob. XVII/6

©San Marco Publications 2023

Rhythm and Meter

Frédéric Chopin
Etude, Op. 10, No. 9

Frédéric Chopin
Waltz, Op. 69, No.1

Giacomo Puccini
Madam Butterfly (One Fine Day)

Lili Boulanger
Nocturne

Rests in Simple Time

A whole rest is used to indicate one complete measure of silence for every time signature except 4/2. In 4/2 meter, the double whole or breve rest is used to indicate a complete measure of silence Figure 10.9.

Figure 10.9

When adding rests to complete a measure of music it is important to show each beat clearly. In Figure 10.10 the first two measures contain one beat of music and are completed with one rest for the remaining beat. In the remaining two measures each incomplete beat is finished before moving on to the next beat.

Figure 10.10

In simple triple meter never join beats two and three into one rest. Beats one and two may be joined or written as two separate rests Figure 10.11.

Figure 10.11

In simple quadruple meter join beats one and two into one rest and join beats three and four into one rest. Never join beats two and three into one rest Figure 10.12.

Figure 10.12

1. Add rests under the brackets to complete each measure.

Rests in Compound Time

Dotted rests are not used in simple meter. They are only used in compound meter and usually equal one beat. Two beats may be joined into one dotted rest to represent the first half or the last half of a measure in compound quadruple meter.

Figure 10.13

In compound meter each beat equals 3 pulses. The first 2 pulses of a beat should be joined into one rest as shown in Figure 10.14 a) and b). The last 2 pulses of a beat should use separate rests as shown in Figure 10.14 c) and d).

Figure 10.14

In compound triple meter beats 1 and 2 may be joined into one rest but do not join beats 2 and 3 into one rest.

Figure 10.15

In compound quadruple time beats 1 and 2 should be joined into one rest. Beats 3 and 4 should be joined into one rest. Do not join beats 2 and 3 into one rest.

Figure 10.16

©San Marco Publications 2023

1. Add rests under the brackets to complete each measure.

❼ 2. Add bar lines to the following excerpts which begin on the first beat of the bar.
❽

Robert Schumann
Carnaval (Eusebius)

Franz Liszt
Hungarian Folksong No. 4

Johannes Brahms
Quintet Op. 111, II

1. Add bar lines according to the time signatures.

❽ 1. Add rests under the brackets to complete the following measures.

Hybrid Meters

Hybrid meters are a combination of simple and compound time. Each measure is made up of dotted (groups of three) and non-dotted (groups of two) notes. Because of this, some beats are longer than others. The top number of a hybrid time signature shows the number of pulses in a measure and the bottom number shows which note gets the pulse.

Hybrid Duple Time

In *hybrid duple time,* the top number of the time signature is always 5. The bottom number may be 4, 8, or 16. There are two beats and five pulses in each measure. This consists of one beat that is worth three pulses and one beat that is worth two pulses. The beats may be grouped as 3 +2 or 2 + 3 as shown in Figure 10.17.

Figure 10.17

Hybrid Triple Time

In *hybrid triple time,* the top number of the time signature may be 7 or 8. The bottom number may be 4, 8, or 16. In Figure 10.18 there are three beats and seven pulses in each measure. This consists of one beat that is worth three pulses and two beats that are worth two pulses each. The beats may be grouped as 3 +2 +2, 2 + 3 + 2 or 2 + 2 + 3.

Figure 10.18

❽ In Figure 10.19 there are three beats and eight pulses in each measure. There are two compound beats and one simple beat. This consists of two beats that are worth three pulses and one beat that is worth two pulses each. The beats may be grouped as 3 +3 +2, 2 + 3 + 3 or 3 + 2 + 3. Do not confuse this with 4/4 which also has 8 eighth notes. 4/4 is grouped into four groups of two eighth notes.

Figure 10.19

Hybrid Quadruple Time

In *hybrid quadruple time,* the top number of the time signature may be 9, 10, or 11. The bottom number may be 4, 8, or 16. There are four beats in each measure. This hybrid meter is less common than the other two. Figure 10.20 shows some of the possibilities for hybrid quadruple time, but many groupings are possible. The following is the beat breakdown for these time signatures:

- One dotted beat and three non-dotted beats equaling 4 beats and 9 pulses. (10.20a.)
- Two dotted beats and two non-dotted beats equaling 4 beats and 10 pulses. (10.20b.)
- Three dotted beats and one non-dotted beat equaling 4 beats and 11 pulses. (10.20c.)

The arrangement of the beats in each time signature can vary.

Figure 10.20

1. Add bar lines according to the time signatures.

❽ 2. Add time signatures to the following two measure examples.

3. Add bar lines according to the time signatures.

❽ • *In hybrid time a whole rest indicates a full measure of silence. as shown in* Figure 10.21.

Figure 10.21

• *When adding rests in hybrid time, show each each beat with one rest when possible.*

In Figure 10.22 there are two beats in each bar. Each beat is indicated with one rest. Measure a) completes the second beat with a quarter rest indicating one beat. Measure b) needs a dotted quarter to complete the first beat. In each measure you can clearly see one 3 pulse beat and one 2 pulse beat.

Figure 10.22

• *If a measure has incomplete beats, finish them before moving on to the rest of the measure.*

In Figure 10.23 a) the first beat is completed with a sixteenth rest and two eighth rests. Do not join pulse two and three into one rest.

• *Use dotted rests to show one complete compound beat.*

Figure 10.23 b) is another option for rest placement. Here, the first beat is treated as the simple beat and the second, compound beat is shown as a dotted rest. Both measures are correct.

• *Combine the first two beats into one rest in hybrid triple. Combine the first two beats and last beats into one rest in quadruple time.*

In Figure 10.23 c) the first two beats of 7/8 are joined into one rest. The last two beats of 11/16 are joined into one rest.
There are many correct ways to complete these bars with rests. It depends where the simple and compound beats occur within the measure.

Figure 10.23

❽ The examples in Figure 10.24 show incorrect and correct rest groupings in a measure. This should help you avoid some common errors when writing rests in hydrid time.

Figure 10.24

⑧ 1. Add rests complete the following measures.

11

Triads

Triad Qualities

The three notes of a triad are known as the root, third and fifth. The quality of a triad is determined by the intervals formed between the root and third and the root and fifth.

Figure 11.1 shows the four different triad qualities. Note the root/quality chord symbols.

Figure 11.1

A *major triad* consist of the intervals of a major 3rd and a perfect 5th above the root.
        G to B is a major 3rd
        G to D is a perfect 5th

A *minor triad* consist of the intervals of a minor 3rd and a perfect 5th above the root.
        G to B♭ is a minor 3rd
        G to D is a perfect 5th

A *diminished triad* consist of the intervals of a minor 3rd and a diminished 5th above the root.
        G to B♭ is a minor 3rd
        G to D♭ is a diminished 5th

An *augmented triad* consist of the intervals of a major 3rd and an augmented 5th above the root.
        G to B is a major 3rd
        G to D♯ is an augmented 5th

1. Provide the root/quality chord symbols for the following triads.

2. Write diminished triads above the following notes.

3. Write augmented triads above the following notes.

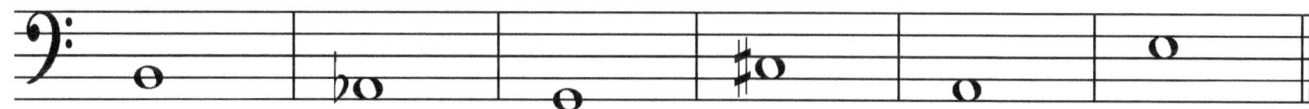

4. Identify the following triads as major, minor, augmented or diminished.

Triad Inversions

Triads may appear in root position and two *inversions*. **Root position triads** have the root as the lowest note. **First inversion triads** have the 3rd as the lowest note. **Second inversion triads** have the 5th as the lowest note. Inverted chords can help make music more interesting. Inversions can create smoother motion between chords. They are used to make a bass line fluid and musical. This type of movement is called **voice leading**. Using root position chords solely can make a disjunct, uneven bass line that jumps around too much. Inversions can make it smoother.

Figure 11.2 shows the three positions of the G major triad.

Figure 11.2

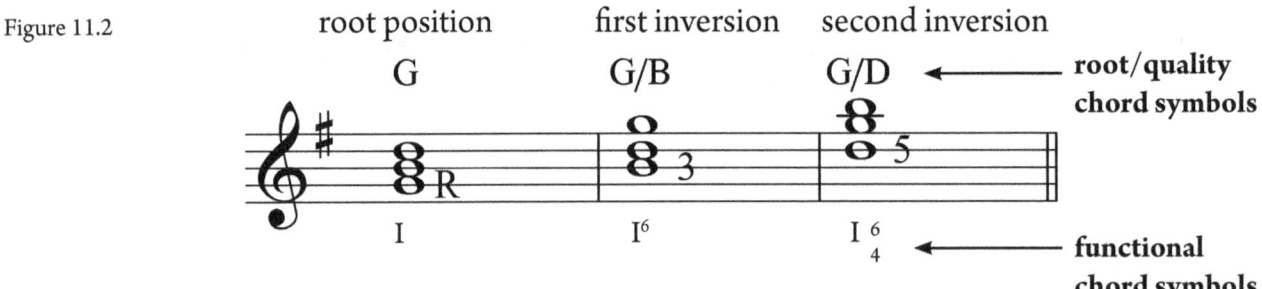

Solving Triads

Figure 11.3

Solving a triad involves stating its root, quality and position. To solve the triad in Figure 10.3:

1. If the triad is not in root position, put it into root position. Figure 11.4 shows that the root is **E**.

Figure 11.4

2. Determine the intervals between the root and 3rd and the root and 5th. In Figure 11.5 E to G is a minor 3rd and E to B♭ is a diminished 5th. This makes the chord quality **diminished**.

Figure 11.5

3. Examine the lowest note of the given triad. In Figure 11.3 it is the 3rd, G. When the 3rd is the lowest note, the position of the triad is **first inversion**. This triad is solved as follows:

Root: E
Quality: diminished
Position: 1st inversion

1. State the root, quality, and position for the following triads.

root: _____ _____ _____ _____ _____ _____
quality: _____ _____ _____ _____ _____ _____
position: _____ _____ _____ _____ _____ _____

root: _____ _____ _____ _____ _____ _____
quality: _____ _____ _____ _____ _____ _____
position: _____ _____ _____ _____ _____ _____

root: _____ _____ _____ _____ _____ _____
quality: _____ _____ _____ _____ _____ _____
position: _____ _____ _____ _____ _____ _____

2. Write the following triads.

F major in root position | G diminished in 1st inversion | D minor in 2nd inversion | C augmented in root position | B♭ minor in 2nd inversion

E major in root position | A diminished in 1st inversion | F♯ diminished in 2nd inversion | B minor in root position | B diminished in 1st inversion

Triads in Open Position

When a triad is written in open position, the notes of the triad are spaced out over more than an octave. Often, one of the notes of the triad is written more than once or **doubled**. The most common note to double is the root. The lowest note of the triad determines the position of the triad.

Figure 11.6 shows triads in open position with root/quality chord symbols.

Figure 11.6

1. State the root, quality and position of the following triads. Add the root/quality chord symbol for each.

root: _____ _____ _____ _____ _____ _____
quality: _____ _____ _____ _____ _____ _____
position: _____ _____ _____ _____ _____ _____

root: _____ _____ _____ _____ _____ _____
quality: _____ _____ _____ _____ _____ _____
position: _____ _____ _____ _____ _____ _____

©San Marco Publications 2023

Triads

Triads Built on the Major and Minor Scale

Figure 11.7 illustrates the major, minor, and diminished triads that occur in the scale of C major. Each triad can be named for the scale degree on which it is built. The triad built on $\hat{1}$, the tonic, is considered the ***tonic triad*** in C major. The triad formed on $\hat{2}$, the supertonic, is considered the ***supertonic triad*** in C major. The triad built on $\hat{3}$ is the ***mediant triad***, etc.

- The root/quality chord symbol for a major triad is an uppercase letter (C, G, etc.).
- The root/quality chord symbol for a minor triad is an uppercase letter and the letter m (Dm, Em, etc.).
- The root quality chord symbol for a diminished triad is the letter and "dim" (Bdim).
- The functional chord symbol a major triad is an uppercase Roman numeral (I, IV).
- The functional chord symbol for a minor triad is a lowercase Roman numeral (ii, iii).
- The functional chord symbol for a diminished triad is a lowercase case Roman numeral with the " ° " symbol (vii°).

Figure 11.7

Major, minor, augmented and diminished triads occur in the harmonic minor scale. Figure 11.8 shows the triads on the A harmonic minor scale. Major triads occur on the dominant ($\hat{5}$) and the submediant ($\hat{6}$). Minor triads occur on the tonic ($\hat{1}$) and subdominant ($\hat{4}$). An augmented triad occurs on the mediant ($\hat{3}$). Diminished triads occur on the super tonic ($\hat{2}$) and the leading tone ($\hat{7}$). The raised leading tone is found in III⁺ and vii°.

- The root/quality chord symbol for an augmented triad is an uppercase letter and "aug' (Caug).
- The functional chord symbol for an augmented triad is an uppercase Roman numeral with the " + " symbol (III⁺).

Figure 11.8

❼ The following table summarizes the triads built on the scale degrees of the major and harmonic
❽ minor scales.

Triad	Major Scales	Harmonic Minor Scales
major	$\hat{1}$, $\hat{4}$, $\hat{5}$	$\hat{5}$, $\hat{6}$
minor	$\hat{2}$, $\hat{3}$, $\hat{6}$	$\hat{1}$, $\hat{4}$
diminished	$\hat{7}$	$\hat{2}$, $\hat{7}$
augmented	none	$\hat{3}$

❼❽ Chord Symbols

Figure 11.9 contains two chords: the leading tone chord and its inversions in A minor, and the subdominant chord and its inversions in G major. Study the notation of the root/quality and functional chord symbols.

Figure 11.9

1. Write all the triads found on the F major scale. Add the functional and root/quality chord symbols for each.

2. Write all the triads found on the D harmonic minor scale. Add the functional and root/quality chord symbols for each.

❼
❽ 3. Name the major key for each triad. Write the scale degree name (tonic, mediant, etc.). Label each triad with functional and root/quality chord symbols.

key: _____ _____ _____ _____ _____ _____
degree: _____ _____ _____ _____ _____ _____

key: _____ _____ _____ _____ _____ _____
degree: _____ _____ _____ _____ _____ _____

4. Name the minor key for each triad. Write the scale degree name (tonic, mediant, etc.). Label each triad with functional and root/quality chord symbols.

key: _____ _____ _____ _____ _____ _____
degree: _____ _____ _____ _____ _____ _____

key: _____ _____ _____ _____ _____ _____
degree: _____ _____ _____ _____ _____ _____

❼ 5. Write the following triads in close position using a key signature for each.
❽
   i.   The dominant triad of E harmonic minor in root position.
   ii. The mediant triad of E♭ major in first inversion.
   iii. The supertonic triad of F♯ harmonic minor in second inversion.
   iv. The subdominant triad of B major in root position.
   v.   The dominant triad of G harmonic minor in first inversion.
   vi. The submediant triad of F major in root position.

6. Write the following triads in close position using accidentals for each. Add the root/quality and functional chord symbols for each chord.

   i.   The leading tone triad of B♭ harmonic minor in root position.
   ii. The submediant triad of F♯ major in second inversion.
   iii. The tonic triad of E♭ harmonic minor in first inversion.
   iv. The dominant triad of F harmonic minor in root position.
   v.   The supertonic triad of E harmonic minor in first inversion.
   vi. The subdominant triad of D major in root position.

7. Write a diminished triad in root position that can be found in the following scales. Use key signatures. Add the root/quality chord symbol to each chord.

i. C major   ii. G major   iii. E harmonic minor   iv. A♭ major   v. A harmonic minor   vi. E major

Chord Symbol Review

Functional Chord Symbols

Functional chord symbols are Roman numerals that are placed under the staff. They identify the root of the chord by the scale degree on which it is built. This symbol also indicates a chords function. For example, V is a dominant function chord, and I is a tonic function chord.

An uppercase Roman numeral indicates a major triad (**I, V**)
A lowercase Roman numeral indicates a minor triad (**ii, iv**)
An uppercase Roman numeral with the plus + sign indicates an augmented triad (**III⁺**)
A lowercase Roman numeral with a degree ° sign indicates a diminished triad. (**vii°**)

Figure 11.10

G major   I   ii   V   vi   vii°

Root/Quality Chord Symbols

Root/quality chord symbols are letters placed above the staff. They identify the root of the chord by its letter name and state the quality of the chord. They do not indicate the key or the function of the chord within the key.

An uppercase letter indicates a major triad (**D, F, B♭**)
An uppercase letter with an 'm' indicates a minor triad (**Dm, Fm**)
An uppercase letter with 'aug' indicates an augmented triad (**Caug**)
A uppercase letter with 'dim' indicates a diminished triad. (**C♯dim**) or (**C♯°**)

Figure 11.11

⑧ Triads Built on Major and Minor Scales

Figure 11.12 contains all of the triads built on the major scale. Major triads occur on $\hat{1}$, $\hat{4}$, and $\hat{5}$. Minor triads occur on $\hat{2}$, $\hat{3}$, and $\hat{6}$. A diminished triad occurs on $\hat{7}$.

Figure 11.12
Major scale

Figure 11.13 contains all of the triads built on the natural minor scale. Major triads occur on $\hat{3}$, $\hat{6}$, and $\hat{7}$. Minor triads occur on $\hat{1}$, $\hat{4}$, and $\hat{5}$. A diminished triad occurs on $\hat{2}$.

Figure 11.13
Natural minor scale

Figure 11.14 contains all of the triads built on the harmonic minor scale. Major triads occur on $\hat{5}$ and $\hat{6}$. Minor triads occur on $\hat{1}$ and $\hat{4}$. Diminished triads occur on $\hat{2}$ and $\hat{7}$. An augmented triad occurs on $\hat{3}$.

Figure 11.14
Harmonic minor scale

1. Write triads on the following scales. Add the functional and root/quality chords symbols.

G major

D harmonic minor

C# natural minor

F harmonic minor

2. For the following triads: 1. Name the **major** key. 2. Write the functional and root/quality chord symbols for each. The first one is done for you.

Bb major   V

Triads

3. Write the following triads using a key signature for each. Add the functional and root/quality chord symbols.

  i. The tonic triad of B major
  ii. The mediant triad of G harmonic minor
  iii. The supertonic triad of E natural minor
  iv. The leading tone triad of B harmonic minor
  v. The dominant triad of C harmonic minor

4. For the following chords: 1. Name the **harmonic minor** key. 2. Write the functional and root/quality chord symbols for each. The first one is done for you.

D minor   vii°

Triad Inversion Review

Triads may appear in root position and two *inversions*. **Root position triads** have the root as the lowest note. **First inversion triads** have the 3rd as the lowest note. **Second inversion triads** have the 5th as the lowest note.

Inverted chords help to make music more interesting. Inversions can create smoother motion between chords. They are used to make a bass line fluid and musical. This type of movement is called **voice leading**. Using root position chords all the time can create a disjunct, uneven bass line that jumps around too much. Inversions can make it smoother.

Figure 11.15 contains the G major triad in root position. The root/quality chord symbol is the letter G, indicating that G is the root and that the quality is major. Since this is the tonic triad in G major, the functional chord symbol is the Roman numeral I. Triads in root position use the Roman numeral alone.

Figure 11.15

Figure 11.16 contains the G major triad in first inversion. The root/quality chord symbol is the letter G followed by a forward slash and the letter B. The B indicates the lowest note of the chord. The functional chord symbol is I^6. The '6' comes from the interval between the lowest note B and the G.

Figure 11.16

Figure 11.17 contains the G major triad in second inversion. The root/quality chord symbol is the letter G followed by a forward slash and the letter D. The D indicates the lowest note of the chord. The functional chord symbol is I^6_4. The $^6_4$ comes from the intervals between the lowest note and the upper notes. D to B is a 6th and D to G is a 4th. Second inversion triads always use $^6_4$ next to the Roman numeral.

Figure 11.17

❽ Figure 11.18 illustrates the chord symbols for the C minor triad in root position and inversions. In root/quality chord symbols, minor triads are indicated with an "m" beside the uppercase letter. In functional chord symbols, minor triads are shown with a lower case Roman numeral.

Figure 11.18

❽ 1. The following triads are in major keys. Name the key and write the root/quality and functional chord symbols for each. The first one is done for you.

2. The following triads are in harmonic minor keys. Name the key and write the root/quality and functional chord symbols for each. The first one is done for you.

❽ 3. Name the key and add functional and root/quality chord symbols to the following chord progressons.

Key:____

Key:____

12

Seventh Chords

The Dominant Seventh Chord - Review

Seventh chords are very common in Western music, and we hear them all the time.

One of the most common seventh chords is the **dominant seventh**. The functional chord symbol for the dominant seventh is V⁷. This means that the chord is built on scale degree $\hat{5}$ (the dominant) and contains the interval of a seventh above the root. A dominant 7th chord contains four notes, the root, 3rd, 5th, and 7th. V⁷ is a major triad with a minor 7th above the root. In other words, the intervals above the root are a major 3rd, perfect 5th, and a minor 7th.

V⁷ contains certain notes, like the leading tone that pull our ear toward the tonic chord.

Figure 12.1 shows V⁷ chords in C and G major and D and E minor. When a key signature is used for these chords, the seventh of V⁷ is automatically a minor seventh. In minor keys, V⁷ like V contains raised $\hat{7}$.

Figure 12.1

❼ Dominant seventh chords sound the same in tonic major and minor keys.

❽ Figure 12.2 shows the dominant seventh chords in F major and F minor. Even though the notation is different, they sound the same and are made up of the same notes.

Figure 12.2

❼ 1. Name the key and write the functional and root/quality chord symbols for the following dominant seventh chords.
❽

7/8 Inversions of the Dominant Seventh

V^7 occurs in root position and three inversions. These are shown in Figure 12.3. Study the root/quality chord symbols.

- If the root is the lowest note, V^7 is in **root position**.
- If the 3rd is the lowest note, V^7 is in **1st inversion**.
- If the 5th is the lowest note, V^7 is is **2nd inversion**.
- If the 7th is the lowest note, V^7 is in **3rd inversion**.

Figure 12.3

When writing the functional chord symbols for inversions of V^7, some of the numbers are omitted.

Figure 12.4 shows the numbers that indicate the intervals that occur above the lowest note. The lower chord symbols are the actual chord symbols that are used for V^7 and its inversions.

Figure 12.4

1. Write dominant seventh chords and their inversion in the following keys using a key signature for each.

G major

C minor

B major

E minor

2. Solve the following dominant chords by stating the two keys, root and position for each.

root: ____ ____ ____ ____ ____ ____
key: ____ ____ ____ ____ ____ ____
key: ____ ____ ____ ____ ____ ____
position: ____ ____ ____ ____ ____ ____

Seventh Chords

root: ____ ____ ____ ____ ____ ____
key: ____ ____ ____ ____ ____ ____
key: ____ ____ ____ ____ ____ ____
position: ____ ____ ____ ____ ____ ____

3. Add accidentals to the following to make dominant seventh chords. Name the major key for each.

key: ____ ____ ____ ____ ____ ____

key: ____ ____ ____ ____ ____ ____

4. State the root, key, and position of the following dominant seventh chords.

root: ____ ____ ____ ____ ____ ____
key: ____ ____ ____ ____ ____ ____
position: ____ ____ ____ ____ ____ ____

root: ____ ____ ____ ____ ____ ____
key: ____ ____ ____ ____ ____ ____
position: ____ ____ ____ ____ ____ ____

The Diminished Seventh Chord

The ***diminished seventh chord*** is built on raised $\hat{7}$ in the minor key.

Figure 12.5 contains the diminished seventh built on raised $\hat{7}$ in A minor. The functional chord symbol is vii°⁷.

Figure 12.5

A minor   vii°⁷

Figure 12.6 shows that this chord consists of a diminished triad with the interval of a diminished 7th above the root of the chord. The root/quality symbol is G♯dim⁷ or G♯°⁷.

Figure 12.6

A minor   vii°   dim 7   vii°⁷

94

©San Marco Publications 2023   Seventh Chords

1. Name the key and write the functional and root/quality chord symbols for the following diminished 7th chords.

Symbol:

Symbol: _____ _____ _____ _____ _____ _____

Key: _____ _____ _____ _____ _____ _____

2. Write diminished 7th chords in the following keys using a key signature for each.

3. Write the following chords using accidentals.

G⁷/D   C♯dim⁷   A♭⁷/G♭   F♯dim⁷   D⁷/F♯   Edim⁷

4. Write the following chords according to the functional chord symbols.

Other Chords

Composers of the late 19th, 20th, and 21st centuries expanded harmonic language and chord structure. The following chords added variety, interest, and dissonant tension to their works.

Chords called **tone clusters**, or **cluster chords** are shown in Figure 12.6. A tone cluster is a chord made up of at least three consecutive tones in a scale. Sometimes they are based on the chromatic scale and are separated by half steps. For example, three adjacent piano keys (such as F, F♯, and G) played simultaneously produce a tone cluster. Tone clusters may also be made up of adjacent diatonic tones. The first clusters were written for the piano, but soon they were being used in music for other mediums. Some modern composers use large keyboard tone clusters called **forearm clusters**. These are performed by slamming the forearm onto the keys. Examples c) and d) show different ways that forearm clusters can be notated.

Figure 12.6

❽ **Polychords** are formed by combining two or more different chords. Only triads and 7th chords are combined to form polychords. Most polychords combine elements of two different keys or modes. Figure 12.7 shows how Ravel used two different chords at the same time to produce a polychord. Here, the right plays a G major triad, and the left hand plays a D♯ minor 7th chord.

Figure 12.7

❽ **Quartal chords** are chords made up of a series of fourths. This is in contrast to more familiar chords (like major, minor, dominant, diminished, augmented) that are built on thirds, (tertian chords). Composers sometimes use these chords in intermittant or brief passages in a composition for their unique effect. Figure 12.8 contains a famous quartal chord used by the composer Alexander Scriabin (1871 - 1915). This chord is known as the **mystic chord**. Scriabin based some of his later works on this quartal chord including his Sonata No. 5, Op. 53. In jazz music quartal chords were made popular by McCoy Tyner (John Coltrane's piano player). They have a jazzy sound and work well in modal music.

Figure 12.8

1. Match each chord with its description.

_____ a tone cluster or cluster chord

_____ vii°⁷ of A harmonic minor

_____ a quartal chord

_____ V⁷ of E minor

_____ a polychord

_____ V$^4_2$ of G major

_____ C augmented triad in 1st inversion

_____ V$^4_3$ of F major

Seventh Chords

13
Cadences

Music is divided into sections or units of various lengths called *phrases*. A phrase is a musical idea, much like a sentence in a story. Most phrases in traditional music are four measures long. A phrase ends with a *cadence*, which is a place of rest in music. A cadence is like the period at the end of a sentence. Cadences consist of two chords which bring a phrase to a close.

There are two types of cadences: ***final*** and ***non-final***. Final cadences bring a phrase to a complete ending. Non-final cadences look forward and do not complete a musical idea. These cadences need another phrase to complete their non-final character.

Figure 13.1 contains two phrases from a Mozart Rondo with a cadence at the end of each. Play this example and listen to the cadences.

The Authentic Cadence

The most frequently used final cadence is the **authentic cadence**. It is the strongest and most conclusive cadence. It consists of the chords V - I or V - i (in minor keys). Figure 13.2 contains two authentic cadences in keyboard style. Notice the following common features of these cadences:

- They occur on the last two notes of the phrase.
- The first chord is on a weaker beat than the second chord.
- The V chord in a minor key contains raised $\hat{7}$.
- In keyboard style, three notes of the chord are placed on the treble staff, and the root of each chord is in the bass staff.
- These cadences are considered **perfect authentic cadences** because they end with the tonic as the top note of the I chord. In the D major cadence, D is the final and top note. In the E minor cadence, E is the final and top note. Ending on the tonic confirms the key and gives the cadence a strong final sound.

Figure 13.2

The cadences in Figure 13.3 are considered **imperfect authentic cadences** because they end with a note other than the tonic on top. The D major cadence ends with the 5th (A) as the final and top note. The E minor cadence ends on the 3rd (G) as the final and top note. These are still final cadences but do not sound as strong and final as a perfect authentic cadence which ends with the tonic as the final and top note.

Figure 13.3

©San Marco Publications 2023

V^7 - I is an authentic cadence. Figure 13.4 contains two authentic cadences using V^7. In the first example in G major, the V^7 chord is complete using all four notes, D F# A C. In the D minor example the V^7 chord is considered incomplete. In this cadence the root is doubled, and the 5th of the chord is left out, A C# G A. Both examples are correct. The root of each chord must always be in the bass.

Figure 13.4

7/8 The Half Cadence

The *half cadence* is a non-final cadence. It ends with the V chord. Ending a phrase on the V chord leaves the music with an open or unfinished sound. For this reason, a piece of music does not end with a half cadence. Half cadences always end on V and never the dominant seventh, since V^7 contains too many strong tones that do not allow a feeling of rest. We will study two half cadences that are shown in Figure 13.5. These two cadences are I - V and IV - V.

Figure 13.5

1. For the following cadences: Name the key, write the functional and root/quality chord symbols and name them as half, perfect authentic, or imperfect authentic.

key: _____

cadence: _____

key: _____

cadence: _____

key: _____

cadence: _____

key: _____

cadence: _____

key: _____

cadence: _____

key: _____

cadence: _____

key: _____

cadence: _____

key: _____

cadence: _____

©San Marco Publications 2023

Writing Cadences

Certain guidelines should be followed when writing cadences. Study the following steps for writing an authentic cadence in E minor.

1. Add the key signature and rests at the beginning of the first measure. Cadences often occur over the bar line with the second chord of the cadence on a stronger beat than the first. The first chord usually occurs in the second half or second part of the first measure on a weaker beat. In Figure 13.6 the key signature of E minor is F sharp. It is placed *before* the time signature. Roman numerals indicating the functional chord symbols of the authentic cadence are placed under the staff (V - i). Since this is 3/4 time a half rest is used at the beginning of the measure and the V chord will be placed on beat 3 of the first measure. There are other options that could be used for rhythm here, but this is effective.

Figure 13.6

2. Write the bass notes for the V and the i chords. In E minor the root of V is B, and the root of i is E. In Figure 13.7 they are written as a quarter note (B) to complete the first measure, and a dotted half note (E) to complete the second measure.

Figure 13.7

❼
❽
3. Write the notes of the V chord in close position on the treble staff. Close position occurs when the notes of the triad are as close together as possible. In E minor V is B-D#-F#. These notes can be in any order as long as they stay in close position. Figure 13.8 uses quarter notes on beat 3 of the first measure for this chord.

Figure 13.8

4. Write the notes of the i chord in the second measure. i in E minor is E-G-B. Keep these notes as close as possible to the notes of the V chord. In Figure 13.9 there is one note that is common to both chords (B). This B is kept in the same place in both chords (here it is the middle note). This note is called the **common tone**. Repeating the common tone in the same place creates smooth movement. This movement of notes from chord to chord is called **voice leading**. The leading tone (D#) rises to the tonic (E). If the leading tone is at the top of the chord, it should rise to the tonic. The F# steps up to G.

Figure 13.9

❼ Writing the half cadence I to V is similar to writing the authentic cadence. There is a common tone
❽ between I and V. Try to repeat it in the same place and move the other voices down a step. In Figure 13.10 the common tone D is the top note of the chords.

Figure 13.10

G major   I   V

The chords of the half cadence IV to V have no common tones. This cadence requires special voice leading. When writing this cadence, it is best to move the 3 upper notes in contrary (opposite) motion to the bass. The bass will rise a step, and the upper voices will fall from the notes of the IV chord to the notes of the V chord. In Figure 13.11, 2 voices step and one voice skips down to the notes of the V chord.

In this cadence, the bass steps up from iv to V (G to A). Do not write this cadence with bass falling a 7th from G down to A. This large melodic interval, a 7th, is not allowed here.

Figure 13.11

D minor   iv   V   iv   V

When writing this cadence, avoid writing two root position chords consecutively as shown in Figure 13.12. This is considered a mistake in voice leading and will be covered more extensively in the next book.

Figure 13.12

D minor   iv   V

1. Write authentic cadences in the following keys. Add functional chord symbols.

A majorC minorD major

B minorB♭ majorF major

2. Write half cadences using I (i) - V in the following keys. Add functional chord symbols.

F minorE majorA♭ major

3. Write half cadences using IV (iv) - V in the following keys. Add functional chord symbols.

F♯ minorC majorD minor

⁷⁄₈ Writing Cadences at the End of a Melody

In this lesson, we will learn to write cadences in keyboard style below a given melody. It is important to remember that this is the melody and you should write the notes of the cadence **under** this melody. If you write above the given part, it will change the melody, and that is wrong!
Follow these steps for writing cadences:

1. Name the key of the melody (the melody below is in G major).
2. Write out the letter names of chords I, IV and V in that key (G major).
   - I   G B D G
   - IV   C E G C
   - V   D F♯ A D
3. Choose the two chords that will harmonize the last two notes of the phrase and create a logical cadence (authentic V - I, plagal IV - I, half I - V, or half IV - V). Here, an authentic cadence, V - I, is the only logical choice for the final melody notes A - G.
4. Write the functional chord symbols (V - I).

Figure 13.13

5. Write the roots of the two chords in the bass staff under the final two melody notes. Here, the bass notes for a V - I cadence are D and G.
6. Complete any empty beats in the measure with rests. In this example, the first two beats of measure 1 need a rest.

Figure 13.14

107

Cadences

7. In the treble clef, add the remaining notes of the chords under each melody note to create a complete chord. Remember that in minor keys V will have raised $\hat{7}$. In Figure 13.15, it is not possible to keep the common tone (D) in the same place, and it is not possible to have the leading tone (F♯) step up to the tonic. This is common when the melody moves from $\hat{2}$ to $\hat{1}$.

Figure 13.15

G major   V   I

Examine the melody in Figure 13.16 a). We have to determine if this melodic fragment is in E♭ major or C minor. It starts on C, but that doesn't mean it is in C minor. If we look at the three primary chords in each key, it will give us an idea.

	E♭ major		C minor
I	E♭ G B♭ E♭	i	C E♭ G C
IV	A♭ C E♭ A♭	iv	F A♭ C F
V	B♭ D F B♭	V	G B♮ D G

When we examine the chords in these two keys, there is only one cadence that fits with the last two melody notes (F - D). That is the half cadence iv - V in C minor. In E♭ major, F - D supports two V chords, and this does not make a cadence. This fragment is in C minor. Figure 13.16 b) shows the half cadence in C minor. Note that there are no common tones and the 3 notes of the iv chord go down to the 3 notes of the V chord. This is in contrary motion to the bass.

Figure 13.16

C minor   iv   V

©San Marco Publications 2023   Cadences

1. For the following melodic fragments: Name the key. Write a cadence at the end in keyboard style. Label the chords with functional chord symbols. Name the cadence as perfect authentic, imperfect authentic, or half.

2. For the following phrases: Name the key. Write a cadence in keyboard style at the end of each phrase. Add functional chord symbols. Name the cadence as perfect authentic, imperfect authentic, or half.

Key:_____ Cadence:_____

Key:_____ Cadence:_____

Key:_____ Cadence:_____

Key:_____ Cadence:_____

Key:_____ Cadence:_____

The Plagal Cadence

The ***plagal cadence*** is a final cadence. In major keys it is IV - I. In minor keys it is iv - i. Like most cadences, it moves from IV on a weak beat to I on a strong beat. Since this cadence does not contain the leading tone, it is not as final sounding as the authentic cadence. The plagal cadence is often heard at the end of church hymns harmonizing the word "Amen." This cadence has its origins in church music but is heard today in music from country to rock.

Figure 13.17 contains plagal cadences in major and minor keys.

Figure 13.17

1. For the following cadences: Name the key, write the functional and root/quality chord symbols and name them as plagal, perfect authentic, imperfect authentic or half.

key: _____   key: _____
  cadence: _____   cadence: _____

key: _____   key: _____
  cadence: _____   cadence: _____

Writing The Plagal Cadence

Certain guidelines should be followed when writing a plagal cadence. Study the following steps for writing an plagal cadence in F major.

1. Add the key signature and rests at the beginning of the first measure. Cadences often occur over the bar line with the second chord of the cadence on a stronger beat than the first. The first chord occurs in the second half or second part of the first measure on a weaker beat. In Figure 13.18 the key signature of F major is B flat. It is placed *before* the time signature. Roman numerals indicating the functional chord symbols of the plagal cadence are placed under the staff (IV - I). Since this is 2/4 time a quarter rest is used at the beginning of the measure and the IV chord will be placed on beat 2 of the first measure. There are other options that could be used rhythmically, but this is effective. Write the bass notes for the IV and I chord in F major.

Figure 13.18

2. Write the notes of the IV chord in close position on the treble staff. Close position occurs when the notes of the triad are as close together as possible. In F major IV is B♭-D-F. These notes can be in any order as long as they stay in close position. Figure 13.19 uses quarter notes on beat 2 of the first measure for this chord.

Figure 13.19

❽ 3. Write the notes of the I chord in the second measure. I in F major is F-A-C. Keep these notes as close as possible to the notes of the IV chord. In Figure 13.20 there is one note that is common to both chords (F). This F is kept in the same place in both chords (here it is the bottom note). This note is called the ***common tone***. Repeating the common tone in the same place creates smooth movement. This movement of notes from chord to chord is called ***voice leading***.

Figure 13.20

The common tone is repeated in the same place.

F major   IV   I

❽ 1. Add key signatures and write plagal cadences in keyboard style in the following keys. Write the functional chord symbols for each cadence.

A major   C minor   D major

G minor   B♭ major   E major

©San Marco Publications 2023   Cadences

Voice Leading

Voice leading was mentioned earlier in relation to writing cadences. Voice leading can be defined in a couple of ways.

1. It can be defined as the way we connect chords, preferably, in the smoothest possible way.
2. It can also be defined as a specific set of rules for how individual voices move from chord to chord. This is most common in four-part writing.

Figure 13.21 contains a chord progression in keyboard style. This progression is clumsy and jumps from one chord to the next.

Figure 13.21

Figure 13.22 contains a much smoother version of the same chord progression. When writing chord progressions, it is best to move to the closest note of the next chord. This progression not only sounds better, but it is easier to play. These chords have common tones that are repeated in the same place between chords. This creates smoother voice leading and a better progression.

Figure 13.22

❽ Cadences in Chorale or Four-Part Style

When cadences are written in *chorale* or *four-part style,* the chords are written in four parts. These four parts make up the four voices of a choir. The four voices are the:

Soprano, Alto, Tenor, and **Bass**

In chorale style, the soprano and alto are written on the treble staff and the tenor and bass are written on the bass staff. Figure 13.23 shows the C major chord written in different positions in chorale style. Note the following:

- The music is written on the grand staff.
- The stems of the soprano and tenor go up.
- The stems of the alto and bass go down.
- The root of each chord is doubled (written twice).
- The space between the soprano and alto and between the alto and tenor cannot exceed one octave. The space between the tenor and bass can be larger than an octave as long as it stays within each voice range.

Figure 13.23

Since chorale writing is for the human voice, we need to know the limits and ranges of each part. Voices are as individual as fingerprints. Individual singers vary, and factors like dynamic level can influence a singers range. Figure 13.24 shows the approximate, average ranges for each voice category. You should keep your writing within these voice ranges.

Figure 13.24

❽ Study the following steps for writing an authentic cadence in chorale style in G minor.

1. Add the key signature and rests at the beginning of the first measure. Add functional chord symbols indicating the authentic cadence (V - i). Write the bass notes for the V and i chord in G minor (Figure 13.25).

Figure 13.25

2. Write the notes of the V chord with doubled root in G minor. V contains the raised leading tone (DF#AD). It might help to write the letter names of the chord under the staff. Be sure to use the correct stem direction and proper spacing between the voices. The space between the top three voices must not exceed one octave (Figure 13.26).

Figure 13.26

3. Write the notes of the i chord with doubled root in G minor. Repeat the common tone (D) in the same voice. Here, it is in the soprano. Move the other voices as smoothly as possible from the V chord to the i chord. In an authentic cadence with a common tone, the remaining two voices step up from the V to the i chord (F# to G and A to B♭) (Figure 13.27).

Figure 13.27

❽ 1. Add the alto and tenor to create authentic cadences in chorale style. (The first one is completed for you).

- It may help to write the letter names of the chord tones under each chord.
- Repeat the common tone in the same voice.
- Move the other voices as closely as possible, preferably by step.
- In minor keys, raise the leading tone in chord V. If the leading tone is in the soprano it must step up to the tonic.
- Be careful of spacing. Do not allow more than one octave space between the top 3 voices.

❽ 2. Complete the following authentic cadences by adding the tonic chord.

❽ Figure 13.28 is a plagal cadence written in chorale style. Writing this cadence is similar to writing the authentic cadence.

- Repeat the common tone in the same voice.
- Move the remaining voices of the IV chord to the nearest available chord tones of the I chord.

In this example the common tone (C) is repeated in the soprano. The bass moves from the root of IV (F) to the root of I (C). The alto and tenor fall a step.

Figure 13.28

C major   IV   I

Figure 13.29 is a half cadence written in chorale style. In this example, the bass moves from the root of I (C) to the root of V (G). The common tone (G) is repeated in the tenor. The remaining voices move down by step. Always try to move to the nearest available chord tone and avoid any awkward leaps within a voice part.

Figure 13.29

C major   I   V

Figure 13.30 contains the half cadence IV - V written in chorale style. There are no common tones in this cadence. When writing this cadence, it is important to move the three upper voices in contrary motion to the bass. The bass steps up, so the soprano, alto, and tenor all move down. Two voices will step down, and one will skip down. Always write the bass in this cadence moving up a step. The alternative is down a 7th, and this melodic interval is awkward.

Figure 13.30

C major   IV   V   this progression

1. Write the following cadences in chorale style.

    a. An authentic cadence in G major
    b. A plagal cadence in C minor
    c. A half cadence (I - V) in B♭ major
    d. An authentic cadence in D minor
    e. A half cadence (iv - V) in A minor
    f. A plagal cadence in E major
    g. A half cadence (i - V) in F♯ minor
    h. An authentic cadence in F minor
    i. A half cadence (IV - V) in D major

2. Name the key. Write an appropriate cadence in chorale style at the end of the following phrases. Add the functional chord symbols and name the cadences.

Key:_____   Cadence:_____

Cadence:_____

Key:_____   Cadence:_____

Cadence:_____

❽ 3. Name the key. Write an appropriate cadence in keyboard style at the end of the following phrases. Add the functional chord symbols and name the cadences.

Key:_____   Cadence:_____

Cadence:_____

Key:_____   Cadence:_____

Cadence:_____

14

Transposition

Transposition Up by Interval

Music may be transposed from one key to another. Melodies in major keys can only be transposed to other major keys and melodies in minor keys can only be transposed to other minor keys.

A melody can be transposed up by a specific interval. For example, you can transpose a melody up a perfect 5th, or a minor 3rd, or a major 2nd, or any other interval. As an example, let us transpose a melody up by the interval of a major 2nd:

1. Determine the key of the original melody. You have to know what key you are starting in before you can determine the key to which you are going. The melody in Figure 14.1 is in E minor.

Figure 14.1

Robert Schumann
Album for the Young (Erster Verlust)

E minor

2. Determine the interval of a major 2nd above E. Figure 14.2 shows that a major 2nd above E is F♯. The new key will be F♯ minor. The key signature of F♯ minor is three sharps. Minor keys can only be transposed to other minor keys.

Figure 14.2

The major 2nd above E is F♯

3. Write the new key signature. In this case, three sharps for F# minor. Rewrite the melody moving every note up a 2nd. The key signature takes care of the quality of the intervals in the transposition. In m.1 of the original, the leading tone D# is an accidental. In the transposition you must show this accidental in the new key. Here, the E is raised to E#, the leading tone of F# minor. Copy everything from the original including the time signature, composer, dynamics, etc. Figure 14.3 contains the original melody transposed into the key of F# minor.

Figure 14.3

Robert Schumann
Album for the Young (Erster Verlust)

Andantino

F# minor

1. In the following examples you are given the original key. Transpose the tonic of these keys by the following intervals. Write the new key signature, the new tonic, and name the new key.

| up a per 5th | up a maj 3rd |
| G major | Bb major |

| up a min 2nd | up a maj 6th |
| A major | Db major |

| up a min 6th | up a per 4th |
| D minor | C# minor |

| up a maj 7th | up a maj 2nd |
| F minor | G minor |

©San Marco Publications 2023   Transposition

2. Name the key of the following melody. Transpose it according to the given intervals. Name the new keys.

Traditional
Drink to Me Only

Key: _____

Transpose up a maj 3rd

Key: _____

Transpose up a per 5th

Key: _____

Transpose up a maj 6th

Key: _____

Transpose up a min 7th

Key: _____

Transpostion Down By Interval

A melody can be transposed down by a specific interval. It is similar to transposing up. Here are the steps for transposing a melody down by the interval of a major 3rd:

1. Determine the key of the original melody. The melody in Figure 14.4 is in C major.

Figure 14.4

Johann Wilhelm Hassler
Minuet, Op. 38, No. 4

C major

2. Determine the interval of a major 3rd below C. Figure 14.5 shows that a major 3rd below C is A♭. The new key will be A♭ major. The key signature of A♭ major is four flats.

Figure 14.5

A major 3rd below C is A♭

3. Write the new key signature, four flats for A♭ major. Rewrite the melody moving every note down a 3rd. This melody has accidentals. Insert the accidentals where they occurred in the original. The first is raised a half step; the second lowered a half step. The original melody used a sharp and a natural. Using the new key signature, a natural and a flat are required to raise and lower these notes. Copy everything from the original including the time signature, composer, tempo, etc. Figure 14.6 contains the original melody transposed into the key of A♭ major.

Figure 14.6

Johann Wilhelm Hassler
Minuet, Op. 38, No. 4

A♭ major

1. In the following examples you are given the original key. Transpose the tonic of these keys by the following intervals. Write the new key signature, the new tonic, and name the new key.

2. Name the key of the following melody. Transpose it according to the given intervals. Name the new keys.

Anton Diabelli
Sonatina, Op. 168, No. 1

Key: _____

Transpose down a maj 2nd

Key: _____

Transpose down a per 4th

Key: _____

Transpose down a min 3rd

Key: _____

Transposition By Key

You may have to transpose to a specific key. The steps for this are similar to transposing by interval. Here, we will transpose a melody into the key of B♭ major.

1. Determine the key of the original melody. The melody in Figure 14.7 is in G major.

Figure 14.7

Franz Schubert
Unfinished Symphony, I

G major

2. The distance from G to B♭ is a minor 3rd. Write the key signature of B♭ major and move every note from the original melody up a 3rd. Copy everything from the original including the time signature, composer, tempo, etc. Follow the normal rules for stem direction. Figure 14.8 contains the original melody transposed into the key of B♭ major.

Figure 14.8

Franz Schubert
Unfinished Symphony, I

B♭ major

1. Name the key of the following melody. Transpose it to the indicated keys. Name the interval of transposition.

Ludwig van Beethoven
Symphony No. 9, IV

Andante maestoso

Key: _____

Down to D major

Interval of transposition: _____

Down to E♭ major

Interval of transposition: _____

Down to B major

Interval of transposition: _____

Up to A major

Interval of transposition: _____

Transposition

❽ Transposing Instruments

Some instruments produce a pitch that is different than the one that is written. These instruments are known as ***transposing instruments***. Suppose you write a piece for trumpet and give a copy to your friend who plays piano, to play along with you. You find the resulting sound is horrible. Why? The trumpet is a transposing instrument, and the piano is not. Not every C and D, or every note for that matter, is the same. It depends on the instrument you are playing.

Concert Pitch

The pitch of a note is created by the vibration of air. These vibrations can be measured and given a frequency number called **hertz** (Hz). Many instruments play in **concert pitch**. This means when they play a note they produce a specific frequency. When you play middle C on the piano, you produce a note with the frequency of 261 hz. This is an exact pitch, and it is associated with concert pitch. Here is a list of some of the instruments that play in concert pitch.

- Piano
- Violin, viola, cello , bass
- Guitar
- Flute, piccolo
- Harp
- Oboe
- Bassoon
- Trombone
- Pitched percussion instruments like marimba, xylophone, timpani
- Tuba

Transposing Instruments - Instruments in B flat

Transposing instruments read the same music and use the same staff, clefs and notes as concert pitch instruments. The difference is when a trumpet plays the note C, it does not register as C according to the hertz scale (261 hz) and it does not match the C on the piano. The trumpet is a B♭ instrument and when it plays C, you hear a B♭ in concert pitch, or it matches the B♭ on the piano. This is what is meant by a transposing instrument. Some B♭ instruments are:

- Trumpet
- Clarinet
- Soprano saxophone

8 Figure 14.9 contains a melody for B♭ trumpet. When it is played, what we hear, concert pitch, is on the second staff. Since we hear B♭ when the trumpet plays C, concert pitch is heard a major 2nd below. In this *Concerto*, a piece for trumpet and orchestra, when the trumpet plays F, we hear E♭. This trumpet concerto is in E♭ major, but the B♭ trumpet plays in F major, a major 2nd higher than concert pitch. The string section, which plays in concert pitch, is playing in E♭ major.

If you have a melody written in concert pitch and want to write it for a B♭ instrument, you have to transpose it up a major 2nd.

If you have a melody written for a B♭ instrument and want to write it in concert pitch, you have to transpose it down a major 2nd.

Figure 14.9

1. The following melody is written for clarinet in B♭. Name the key and transpose it into concert pitch. Name the new key.

2. The following melody is written in concert pitch. Name the key and transpose it for trumpet in B♭. Name the new key.

Johann Nepomuk Hummel
Trumpet Concerto, III

Key: _____

Key: _____

3. The following melody is written for clarinet in B♭. Name the key and transpose it into concert pitch. Name the new key.

Wolfgang Amadeus Mozart
Symphony No. 40, Minuet

Key: _____

Key: _____

Transposing Instruments - Instruments in F

Two instruments transpose in the key of F:

- French horn
- English horn

They both transpose in the same manner, a fifth away. Music for these instruments must be transposed down a perfect 5th to get to concert pitch. (See Figure 14.10) In other words, a melody in concert pitch must be written up a perfect 5th to sound correct when played by an F instrument. A melody written for an F instrument must be transposed down a perfect 5th to sound correct at concert pitch.

Figure 14.10

French/English horn plays:

We hear at concert pitch:

1. The following melody is written for horn in F. Name the key and transpose it into concert pitch. Name the new key.

Wolfgang Amadeus Mozart
Concerto for Horn K. 447, III

Key: _____

Key: _____

2. The following examples are in concert pitch. Name the keys and rewrite each one for the instrument indicated. Name the new keys.

Wolfgang Amadeus Mozart
Allegro, K.312

Allegro

Key: _____

Clarinet in B♭

Key: _____

French Horn

Key: _____

Antono Vivaldi
The Four Seasons, Spring

Largo

Key: _____

English Horn

Key: _____

Trumpet in B♭

Key: _____

©San Marco Publications 2023 — 136 — Transposition

15
Score Types

8 Score is a common term for notated music. There are several types of scores which we will discuss in this lesson.

Piano Score

A piano score is written on the grand staff. It consists of the treble and the bass staff joined by a bracket or brace. The bar lines go through both staves. The tempo indication is placed at the beginning of the staff. The key signature comes after the clef and is followed by the time signature. Dynamics (fp) are placed between the two staves. Figure 15.1 is a piano score.

Figure 15.1

Orchestral Score

An orchestral score has staves for all the instruments that are playing. The instruments are placed in the following order: woodwinds, brass, percussion (timpani), strings. Each section is divided with a bracket on the left side. the instruments are placed on the staff from highest to lowest in each family. The instrument names are usually written in Italian. On this score, the English translations are included. There is one tempo mark at the beginning, and each part receives its own dynamic marking.

Figure 15.2

⁸ Vocal Scores

Short Score

Short score, which is sometimes called condensed score, looks a little like piano score but there are some differences. This score consists of the treble and bass staves joined at the beginning by a line and a brace. In vocal music, the bar lines do not run through the entire staff.

This score is written for the four voices of a choir: soprano, alto, tenor, and bass. The soprano and alto parts are written on the treble staff, and the tenor and bass parts ware written on the bass staff.

Stem direction rules are different in short score. The soprano stems go up, and the alto stems go down in the treble clef. The tenor stems go up, and the bass stems go down in the bass clef. This separates the parts, and each singer can clearly see their line. The text to be sung is placed between the staves. Figure 15.3 is an example of a short score.

Figure 15.3

Chorale No. 293
Was Gott tut, das ist wohlgetan

Johann Sebastian Bach

⑧ Modern Vocal Score

Modern vocal score is an example of **open score**. In open score, each part gets its own staff. The three upper parts are written on treble staves. The bass part is written on the bass staff. The tenor part is written one octave higher on the treble staff. Each part receives the text to be sung.

Figure 15.4 is the chorale from Figure 14.3 written in modern vocal score.

Figure 15.4

Chorale No. 293
Was Gott tut, das ist wohlgetan

Johann Sebastian Bach

⁸ String Quartet Score

String quartet score is an open score. The instruments in this score are first violin, second violin, viola, and cello (violoncello). The violin parts are written using two treble staves. The viola is written using the alto staff and the cello is written using the bass staff.

Figure 15.5 is written in string quartet score. The instruments are abbreviated as:

> Vl. I
> Vl. II
> Vla
> Vc

Figure 15.5

Writing in Short and Open Score

There are few things to consider when transcribing a passage from short to open score or vice versa. The example in Figure 14.6 is in short score. The stem direction goes up for soprano and tenor and down for alto and bass. The tempo is written once, the dynamic sign is written once, and the fermata is written above the soprano and below the bass.

Figure 15.6

Figure 15.7 shows the same example written in open score for SATB. Normal rules of stem direction are followed. The tempo is written once at the top, and each part receives a dynamic marking. Each part receives a fermata. All four voices are lined up evenly on the score.

Figure 15.7

❽ In short score, the ties in the soprano and tenor parts curve upwards, and the ties in the alto and bass parts always curve downwards. Figure 14.8 contains ties in the soprano and alto.

Figure 15.8

In open score, ties are always written on the opposite side of the note to the stem.

Figure 15.9

❽ Sometimes, two parts can sing an identical note or a "unison," or they may sing the interval of a second.

Study the soprano and alto parts in Figure 15.10. On beat one they are singing the same G. On beat two the soprano has a G, and the alto has the F directly below it.

Figure 15.10

❽ These parts are transcribed into short score in Figure 15.11. In a short score, a unison is shown by writing one note-head with two stems. One stem points up, and the other points down.

For the interval of a major second on beat two, the F in the alto is moved slightly to the right. This allows both notes to be seen.

Figure 15.11

1. Write the following passage in open score for a string quartet.

Johann Sebastian Bach
Chorale no. 67: Freu'dich sehr, o meine Seele

Score Types

2. Write the following passage in modern vocal score.

Johann Sebastian Bach
Das walt' mein gott

3. Write the following passage in short score.

Ludwig van Beethoven
String Quartet Op 18, No. 1

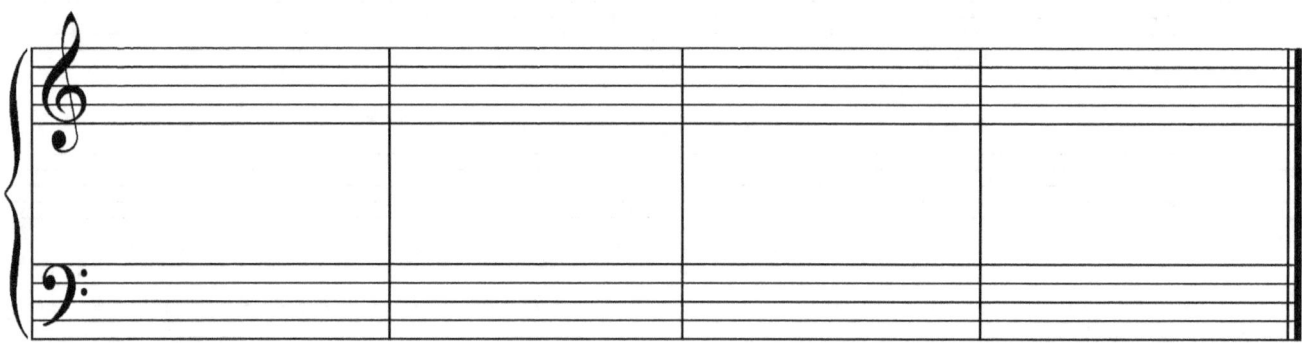

4. Write the following passage in string quartet score.

Franz Joseph Haydn
String Quartet Op 76, No. 3

©San Marco Publications 2023

Score Types

5. Write the following passage in short score.

Johann Sebastian Bach
O Haupt Voll und Wunden

16
Melody Writing

Review - Implied Harmony

The notes of a melody can imply or suggest certain chords that may go along with it. This is called the ***implied harmony***. Figure 16.1 contains the i, iv, and V chords in D minor.

Figure 16.1

Chords can be used with a melody if they contain the same notes as those found in the melody. Study the implied harmony for the melody in Figure 16.2.
The D, F and A in m.1 suggest the i chord in D minor. This is the opening measure. Most pieces begin with the tonic chord. This helps to establish the key or tonality.
The G and B flat in m.2 imply the iv chord in D minor.
The A and C sharp in m.3 imply the V chord in D minor.
The final measure contains a D implying i and forming an authentic cadence with V in the previous measure.
Musical phrases must make harmonic sense and this includes implying a logical cadence at the end of the phrase.

Figure 16.2

❼ Figure 16.3 contains the previous melody with the implied harmony realized in the bass clef.
❽

Figure 16.3

❼ 1. For the following melodies: Name the key. State the implied harmony by adding functional
❽ (Roman numeral) chord symbols.

Key:_____

Key:_____

Key:_____

Key:_____

Key:_____

©San Marco Publications 2023   Melody Writing

Non-Chord Tones

A melody may have notes that are not part of the implied harmony. These are called **non-chord tones**. Non-chord tones always have a function or a reason for being. We do not write a note that is not part of the underlying harmony unless we can explain its function. In this level, we will study two different non-chord tones.

The Passing Tone (PT)

Non-chord tones are classified according to how they are approached and left. A **passing tone** is a non-chord tone that is approached and left by step. It fills in the interval of a 3rd. In Figure 16.4 (a), all of the notes are part of the implied harmony (I). They are chord tones. In (b), there are two notes that are not part of the I chord. These are non-chord tones. The notes D and F are not part of the I chord in C major (C-E-G). These two notes fill in the interval of a 3rd between C and E and E and G. Each non-chord tone is approached and left by step. The D is approached by step from C and is left by step to E. The F is approached by step from E and left by step to G.

When we analyze music, non-chord tones are circled and marked with an abbreviation to indicate their function. Here, PT is used for passing tone.

Figure 16.4

The Neighbor or Auxilliary Tone (NT)

A **neighbor tone** sometimes called an **auxiliary tone**, is a non-chord tone that moves a step above or a step below two common tones. It is approached and left by step. Figure 16.5 contains two neighbor tones. In this measure, the harmony could imply IV in C major (F-A-C). Anything that is not an F, A, or C is a non-chord tone. The two G's are not part of this chord. The first is an upper neighbor to the note F. The second is a lower neighbor to the A. They are circled and labeled NT to indicate their function.

Figure 16.5

7. Figure 16.6 is based on the melody from Figure 15.2. Here, the addition of passing tones and a neighbor
8. tone add movement and interest to the original melody. Play and compare both.

Figure 16.6

1. For the following melodies: Name the key. Add functional chord symbols stating the implied harmony. Circle and label any non-chord tones.

Key:_____

Key:_____

Key:_____

Key:_____

Key:_____

©San Marco Publications 2023

2. Name the keys of the following melodies. Rewrite them adding passing and neighbor tones where appropriate. Add functional chord symbols stating the implied harmony.

Key:_____

Key:_____

Key:_____

Key:_____

7/8 Melodic Structure - The Parallel Period

A ***period*** is usually eight measures long and contains two four-measure phrases, called antecedent and consequent.

Antecedent and consequent phrases are common in music. The first phrase acts as a question, often ending on an unstable tone ($\hat{2}$ or $\hat{7}$), which requires an answer. The second phrase provides the answer and usually ends on a stable tone ($\hat{1}$ or $\hat{3}$).

The melody in Figure 16.7 consists of two phrases that are almost the same. The difference is the ending. The first phrase ends on an unstable pitch ($\hat{2}$). The second phrase ends on a stable pitch ($\hat{1}$). Since the second phrase uses the same melody with a slight alteration, the two phrases are labeled **a** and **a¹**. This type of melody construction, with two similar melodies, is called a ***parallel period***. In this example, each phrase begins with an anacrusis or pickup. This is common and helps create unity in the music.

Figure 16.7

7/8 Cadences

Phrases end in cadences. In Figure 16.7, the unstable pitch $\hat{2}$ at the end of the first phrase implies a half cadence.

The second phrase ends on the stable pitch $\hat{1}$, implying an authentic cadence. It is important that the notes at the end of a melodic phrase imply a logical cadence.

The Contrasting Period

The parallel period consists of two similar four measure phrases labeled: **a** and **a¹**. The labels **a** and **a¹** indicate the similarity between the two phrases.

The ***contrasting period*** consists of two differing four measure phrases labeled: **a** and **b**.
The melodic material in the second (consequent) phrase is different than **a**. For this reason, it is labeled "**b**".

Study and play the melody in Figure 16.8. There are two phrases: an antecedent and a consequent. Each phrase begins with an anacrusis. However, section **a** and section **b** differ. Section **b** uses the same rhythm as section **a**, but it contains new melodic material. This type of melody, with two differing phrases, is a contrasting period.

Figure 16.8

In Figure 16.9, the consequent phrase **b,** contains a contrasting melody based on a descending melodic sequence using rhythm from m.1. A ***melodic sequence*** is the repetition of a melodic idea at a higher or lower pitch.

Figure 16.9

©San Marco Publications 2023   Melody Writing

❼ You will be asked to compose the consequent or "**b**" phrase of a contrasting period. There are many
❽ ways to do this. The most important point is to try and hear in your mind what you have written. When you write an exam, you will not have access to an instrument. However, in the early stages, when you are practicing writing melodies, it may be a good idea to play them on your instrument to see whether you have written the sounds that you intended.

Writing a melody is more than creating patterns of notes on paper. It is about your creativeness and imagination. The most important features of a good melody are its rhythmic organization and the shapes produced by the pitches of the notes.

Here are some ideas to help you create good melodies.

1. When planning the rhythm of a consequent phrase look at the rhythm of the given (antecedent) phrase. Try to base your melody on related rhythms. The rhythm of the consequent phrase in Figure 16.9 is based on one measure of rhythm found in the antecedent phrase. Introducing an unusual or foreign rhythmic figure in the consequent phrase may make it sound like it does not belong to the complete period.

2. In Figure 16.9, the antecedent phrase begins with an anacrusis. The consequent phrase also begins with an anacrusis. This is very common and creates rhythmic unity.

3. A melody should have a sense of direction or shape. It may move to a high point or climax and then down again. Try not to circle around the same few notes.

4. Scalewise motion is good. A leap is the interval of a 3rd or more. Leaps are good for contrast, but try to avoid too many of them because the melody could lose its shape.

5. Avoid dissonant intervals. In major keys, an augmented 4th occurs between $\hat{4}$ and $\hat{7}$ and should be avoided. You can write a diminished 5th, but try to leave this interval to a melody note that is within its compass. Figure 16.10 illustrates a melody using these intervals.

Figure 16.10

6. The final note of the first or antecedent phrase is often an unstable scale degree like $\hat{2}$ or $\hat{7}$. This implies a half cadence. A logical cadence must be implied at the end of a phrase. End the consequent phrase on a stable tone, preferably the tonic. This implies an authentic cadence. A melody that ends on the tonic is very strong and reinforces the tonality or key. This final tonic note is often approached from below by scale degree $\hat{7}$, or from above, by scale degree $\hat{2}$. Study and play the phrase endings in Figure 16.11.

Figure 16.11

1. For following antecedent phrases: Name the key. Write a consequent phrase creating a **contrasting parallel period**. End on a stable scale degree. Mark the phrases. Name the implied cadences at the end of each phrase. Label each phrase **a** and **b**.

Key:_____   Cadence:_____

Cadence:_____

Melody Writing

1. For the following given consequent (a) phrases:
   - Name the key.
   - Write an antecedent phrase (b) creating a contrasting period.
   - Use the suggested implied harmony as a guideline. Alter it if you wish, but end the phrase with a logical authentic cadence. It may help to end on $\hat{1}$, approached from a step below ($\hat{7}$-$\hat{1}$) or a step above ($\hat{2}$-$\hat{1}$).

❽ 2. For the following melodic fragments:

- Name the key.
- Complete the consequent (a) phrase, ending on an unstable scale degree ($\hat{2}$, $\hat{7}$, $\hat{5}$).
- Write an antecedent (b) phrase creating a contrasting period ending on a stable scale degree ($\hat{1}$).
- State the implied harmony using functional chord symbols.

Key:_____

Key:_____

Key:_____

17
History

History Level 7

The Romantic Era (ca 1825 - 1900)

The **Romantic era** comes after the Classical era. This period covers most of the 19th century, from about the years 1825 to 1900.

Romanticism was a cultural movement that started in Europe. This movement influenced philosophical thinking, literature, music, and art.

Romantic music was influenced by the literature and painting of the era. It was marked with deep emotional expression. Romantic music expressed strong feelings through music. It was more pictorial than earlier music and often attempted to describe something, perhaps a scene in nature, a poem, a story, or a particular feeling. Music that has a literary or pictorial association is called ***program music***. Pieces were often given descriptive titles like Album Leaf, Nocturne, Impromptu, Humoresque, Intermezzo, Arabesque, Papillons.

A few of the composers from this period include Franz Schubert, Frédéric Chopin, Franz Liszt, Robert Schumann, Johannes Brahms, Felix Mendelssohn, Edvard Grieg, Piotr Ilyich Tchaikovsky, Guisseppe Verdi, Georges Bizet, and many more.

Felix Mendelssohn (1809 - 1847)

Felix Mendelssohn was born in 1809 in Hamburg, Germany to a wealthy family with parents who encouraged him to be a musician.

Mendelssohn was the most celebrated child prodigy since Mozart. He began taking piano lessons from his mother when he was 6 and made his first public concert appearance at the age of 9. As a child, he composed extensively, writing five short operas and 11 symphonies by the time he was in his teens.

Mendelssohn came from a musical family. His sister Fanny was also an excellent pianist and composer. The two of them put on Shakespeare's comedy A Midsummer Night's Dream to entertain family and friends and played all of the characters. Mendelssohn's music for A Midsummer Night's Dream describes the plot and many characters in the play.

Mendelssohn's grandfather was the Jewish philosopher Moses Mendelssohn. Being Jewish in Germany was difficult for the Mendelssohn family. They lived at a time when there were specific taxes and laws that only applied to Jews. Because of this discrimination against Jewish people, (known as anti-Semitism), Mendelssohn's father decided to convert to Christianity and changed the family name to Mendelssohn-Bartholdy.

Mendelssohn can be given credit for reviving the music of Johann Sebastian Bach which was largely forgotten by the 19th century. In 1829 he conducted a performance of Bach's St. Matthew Passion, a work for orchestra, choir and soloists. The concert was so successful it started a renewed and lasting appreciation for the music of Bach.

Mendelssohn traveled extensively. His trips to other countries inspired some of his best music. The Italian and Scottish symphonies were inspired by his travels and are two examples of *exoticism*. Exoticism is a term used to describe music that evokes the atmosphere of far-off lands or cultures. Mendelssohn, a German, wrote symphonies inspired by lands that were not part of his heritage.

Mendelssohn died in 1847 at the age of 38 after suffering from ill health. His life was short. However, he managed to distinguish himself as one of the greatest composers of the Romantic period.

Overture to a Midsummer Nights Dream

A German translation of the Shakespeare play " A Midsummer Nights Dream" became part of the Mendelssohn's library in 1826. Felix loved it and wrote this overture in 1827 when he was just 17 years old.

The genre of this composition is **concert overture**. A concert overture is a single movement concert piece for symphony orchestra based on a literary idea. Overture to a Midsummer Nights Dream is written for two flutes, two oboes, two clarinets, two bassoons, two horns, two trumpets, ophicleide, timpani, and strings. An ophicleide is a bass brass instrument with keys that was eventually replaced by the tuba.

A concert overture is considered ***program music***. Program music is music that has a literary or pictorial association. It has an extra-musical meaning and evokes images or ideas.

A Midsummer Nights Dream is based on the Shakespeare play of the same name. It involves fairies, love potions, and some very bizarre ideas. The play ends by telling the audience it was nothing but a dream.

A concert overture is a romantic piece, but Mendelssohn uses a few classical elements like sonata form. Sonata form consists of three sections:

1. **The Exposition**. In this section, the composer introduces themes that will be used throughout the composition. There are usually two contrasting themes, and this section ends in a new key (the dominant or relative major).
2. **The Development**. In this section, the composer develops the themes from the exposition. This may be done by exploring motives and sequences based on the themes, but the main feature of the development is the exploration of different keys.
3. **The Recapitulation.** Here, the themes from the exposition return in the tonic key. This section remains in the tonic key and often ends with a ***coda***. Coda means "tail" in Italian. A coda is a concluding section of a piece of music. Its length can vary, but it adds a final embellishment to the end of a composition.

Mendelssohn's overture is in the key of E major, and it begins with an introduction before the exposition starts. This consists of four magical chords that give you the impression that you are in a dream. These chords are played by the wind instruments. They invite the listener to a magical forest near Athens where the play is set.

The example below contains the first theme in the exposition. This theme is played by the violins and depicts the fairies scurrying through the woods. It is written in the tonic minor, E minor.

A fanfare-like transition leads to the second theme. The first part shown below is played by the full orchestra and portrays the lovers. The second line shown below paints a musical picture of the character named Bottom after Puck's magic has turned him into a donkey. His "hee-hawing" is played by the strings.

The exposition is followed by the development section and the recapitulation. The overture ends with the same four magical chords with which it started. Mendelssohn starts the piece like a dream and completes it in the same way, interpreting Shakespeare's play perfectly.

Frédéric Chopin (1810 - 1849)

Frédéric Chopin was born on March 1, 1810, in Żelazowa Wola, Poland. His father was French, and his mother was Polish. His mother introduced him to the piano. He started his musical education at 6, composed his first work at 7, and made his first appearance on stage at 8 years of age. Chopin was devoted to the piano and composed almost exclusively for this instrument.

When Chopin was 20, he left Poland for France and lived the rest of his life in Paris. However, his love and devotion for Poland never died. He carried a small silver box filled with Polish earth when he left Poland. This box was buried with him when he died in Paris in 1849. His heart was put in an urn and placed in the Church of the Holy Cross in Warsaw, Poland.

Chopin's music is infused with his love and devotion to Poland. Some of this influence can be seen in his piano works. He wrote mazurkas and polonaises, based on Polish folk dances.

The majority of his solo pieces are composed in smaller forms and have an improvisatory sound. These include 20 nocturnes, 25 preludes, 17 waltzes, 15 polonaises, 58 mazurkas and 27 etudes. Chopin also wrote larger forms, including the scherzo, the ballade (a genre he invented), and the sonata. The four Ballades and the two Sonatas are among his most significant compositions.

Chopin had a love for opera and the music of opera composer Vincenzo Bellini. Much of his piano music is written in a style called *bel canto*. Bel Canto style translates to "beautiful singing style." Chopin's piano music is noted for its beautiful singing lines and melodies. His music is also known for its virtuosity and its advanced treatment of harmony and rhythm.

Elements in Chopin's Music

Rubato: All of Chopin's music employs rubato. This is an expressive and rhythmic freedom achieved by speeding up and slowing down the tempo of a piece at the discretion of the performer.

Harmony: Unlike composers of the past, Chopin's chords don't just function as a set of tensions and resolutions. Many have a unique, individual, colorful sound. Chopin discovered that dissonance, which creates tension and traditionally requires resolution, can be beautiful by itself. His music often contains chromaticism, unusual modulations, and sudden key changes.

Nationalism: Music based on a composers country is nationalistic. Polish culture, folk songs, and rhythms influence Chopin's music.

Etude Op. 10 No. 12 (Revolutionary)

The term *etude* is used to describe a piece of music that focuses on refining and training a specific aspect of a performers technique. Etudes are sometimes referred to as **studies**. Many etudes are just repetitions of note patterns and lack real musicality. Chopin's etudes are different. He was the first composer to pioneer the etude as an actual art form. He wrote 27 etudes for piano. Each of the Chopin etudes not only trains a specific technical area but also tells an emotional story. They are anything but repetitive, dry, technical exercises. This musical approach to the etude continued through the Romantic period and other composers, notably Franz Liszt, wrote in this genre.

Chopin's etudes cover many areas of technique, from arpeggios to octaves, but all are designed to develop a legato style of playing.

The Etude in C minor Op. 10, No. 12 is one of Chopin's most recognized compositions. The genre of this etude is **solo piano piece**. This piece has been given the programmatic title "Revolutionary Etude." It was composed after Chopin heard of Poland's failure in its rebellion against Russia. Chopin never gave titles like this to his compositions, almost always preferring to refer to them by opus and number. He probably did not come up with this title, and actually may have disapproved of it. This nickname might be attributed to an editor or fan of his music.

Most of the technical difficulty in this etude is in the left hand, which has rapid runs, arpeggios, and broken chords. It is in ternary (ABA) form.

A is mm. 1 - 28
B is mm. 29 - 42
A is mm. 43 - 84

The opening eight measures act as in introduction to the main theme which begins in m. 10.

Find and listen to a recording of this etude on the internet.

The Modern Era (ca 1900 - present day)

In the Modern Era (1900 - present), composers followed traditional musical ideas but used their own creative approach. This resulted in freedom in all areas, including melody, rhythm, and chord progression. The development of audio recording technology, computers, and the internet was also very important to the development of modern music.

Music from the Modern era has a lot of variety. There are a number of different "schools" of composition. Many composers had their own way of thinking about composition, and how to compose in new and different ways. These new ways created new genres (types of music) that have names ending in "ism." Examples of these are impressionism, serialism, neoclassicism, expressionism, minimalism, and post-modernism. The Modern period also includes jazz, world music (music from non-European cultures), and electronic music.

Igor Stravinsky (1882 - 1971)

Igor Stravinsky was born in Oranienbaum, Russia. His father was an opera singer and his mother a pianist. Stravinsky began taking piano lessons at age 9. After high school, his parents convinced him to study law. One of his fellow law students was the son of the famous Russian composer Nikolai Rimsky-Korsakov. This connection allowed Stravinsky to take music composition lessons from the great composer.

Stravinsky became famous in the early 1900s when he wrote music for the Russian Ballet, including *The Firebird, Petrushka,* and *The Rite of Spring.* He fled Russia with the outbreak of World War I and took his family to Switzerland. He missed Russia during this period, and he composed music based on Russian Folklore as well as music influenced by jazz.

In 1920 Stravinsky moved his family to Paris where he lived for 20 years. Following the deaths of his wife and a daughter from tuberculosis, in 1939, he moved to the United States and became an American citizen. He died in New York City in 1971, having written more than 100 works.

Petrushka

Petrushka is a **ballet** by Igor Stravinsky. Ballet is an art form that consists of music, dancing, and scenery to convey a story or theme. Petrushka is composed for an orchestra with a large percussion section including a piano.

Until 1920, Stravinsky's works were deeply connected to his Russian heritage. The most famous ballet to build upon this Russian pride is Petrushka, composed in 1911. In this ballet, Stravinsky incorporated themes from Russian folk songs.

Petrushka was first performed in 1911 in Paris by the Ballets Russes. The story is based on traditional Russian folklore and features a puppet named Petrushka. Stravinsky's version of the story involves three puppets brought to life by a magician: Petrushka, a Ballerina, and the Moor. Petrushka, a wild and rebellious jester, falls in love with the Ballerina, but she only has eyes for the handsome, arrogant Moor. The Moor kills Petrushka in a duel, but Petrushka's ghost reappears to haunt the magician who brought him to life.

Petrushka is a complicated work that does not follow the conventional rules of tonality. Harmonically and rhythmically it moves away from traditional compositional rules by using unusual scales, polychords, and polyrhythms.

Petrushka has a pitch center (C), but it does not use the conventional pitch relationships that are seen in the major and minor tonal system. Instead, Stravinsky uses the octatonic scale as a basis for this work. An octatonic scale is based on alternating whole steps and half steps. In this case: C, C#, D#, E, F#, G, A, A#, C.

Stravinsky uses **polyrhythms** in Petrushka. Polyrhythm involves using two or more differing rhythms at the same time. For example, one musical line may be playing in 3/4 time, while another line is playing in 4/4 time.

Polytonality is also a feature of Petrushka. A polychord is a single chord made up of two or more different chords played at the same time. For example, if you take a C major chord and a D major chord and stack one on top of the other:

C major: C E G
D major: D F# A

The result is a chord that looks like the chord below.

Petrushka does not have the traditional tonic/dominant relationship found in tonal music. A traditional piece of music in C might feature a lot of movement from C (the tonic) to G (the dominant). This tonal relationship is very consonant (pleasing). Stravinsky replaces the dominant chord with a chord based on the augmented fourth. The interval from C to F# is an augmented fourth, and this relationship is very dissonant (displeasing).

Petrushka moves between the two chords: C major (C, E, G) and F# major (F#, A#, C#). The juxtaposition of these two chords represents Petrushka's bold and brash character. There are times when they meet, creating the polychord C, C#, E, F#, G, A# shown below in a. Since it is used so much in the music, this chord has come to be known as the "Petrushka chord." Example b. shows how this chord is derived from notes of the octatonic scale.

a.

b.

Rondo Form

Form in music is the way a composition is organized. The form is determined by several factors, including changes of key, when new musical material occurs, and when former musical material is restated.

Petrushka is in **rondo form**. In rondo form, musical material stated at the beginning of the piece keeps returning. This opening music can be called the **theme** or the **refrain**. Between statements of the theme or refrain, there are **episodes**. An episode is musical material that is different from the theme.

The theme, or refrain, of a rondo, is the first main melody or musical material that occurs in the piece. It will establish the key of the piece, and the theme will most often be played in this same key. Since it is the first material we hear in the piece, we label this part of the music the A-section.

The episodes usually differ in melody, in musical character, or in key from the theme. We label the first episode the B-section. For each different episode that occurs in the music, we use a different label, such as 'C,' 'D,' and so on.

In rondo form, the theme or A section will keep returning after every episode. One example of rondo form would be ABACA. The theme, or A-section, will always return after every episode.

The length of a Rondo varies depending on the number of sections it contains. ABACA and ABABA are examples of 5 part Rondo forms because they have a total of five sections. ABACABA and ABACADA are examples of 7 part Rondo forms.

Petrushka is a 7 part Rondo with its structure being ABACABA.

Duke Ellington (1899 - 1974)

Edward Kennedy "Duke" Ellington was born in Washington, D.C. on April 29, 1899. He was an American pianist, bandleader, and composer, most often known for his work with big band swing music. Ellington was a talented pianist but is famous for his big bands. These were orchestra-sized jazz bands that played dance music.

As an African-American composer working in Harlem, Ellington was an important part of the Harlem Renaissance, a period of artistic and intellectual production that took place in Harlem, New York in the 1920s. The greatest jazz players in history turned up to play with Ellington, and he wrote music to showcase their talents.

Throughout his life, Duke Ellington helped make jazz music successful throughout the world. He thought the term 'jazz' was not appropriate for his music because it was limiting. He referred to his music as 'American music.'

By the time of his death in 1974, he had composed thousands of original pieces of music including "It Don't Mean a Thing if It Ain't Got That Swing," "Sophisticated Lady," "Mood Indigo," "Solitude," and "Satin Doll."

To this day, Ellington is one of the most prolific composers and has personally contributed more to jazz music than any other person in history.

Jazz

Jazz is a music genre that has its origins in African American communities in the late 19th and early 20th centuries. Major features of jazz are improvisation and rhythm. Jazz musicians express themselves through ***improvisation***, requiring them to be inventive and create music on the spot. They do this by embellishing the melody or by changing melodies rhythmically. A key element of jazz is ***rhythmic syncopation***, which is when accents occur on the off-beat. Some jazz is ***polyrhythmic***, which is when multiple, contrasting rhythms occur at the same time.

Blues

Blues is a musical form started in the United States at the beginning of the 20th century. The blues are derived from spirituals, work songs, and field-hollers by African slaves. The first blues songs originated near the Mississippi River and were called the Delta blues. As African Americans moved throughout the United States, they took the blues with them and developed regional styles of this genre. Blues are the foundation of almost every American musical form in the 20th century, including jazz, rock and roll, hip-hop, and rap.

Twelve-bar Blues

12-bar blues progressions are organized into three 4-bar sections: four bars of the I chord, two bars each of the IV and I chords, and one bar of V, one bar of IV, and two bars of I (or one bar of I and one bar of V).

The piece below is the 12-bar blues in C. The right hand is based on the C blues scale.

Mark Sarnecki

Koko

Duke Ellington wrote *Koko* in 1940. This piece is inspired by drumming from African religious ceremonies Ellington heard in New Orleans. He wrote it for his big band which consisted of piano, drums, guitar, trumpets, trombones, clarinets, and saxophones. Koko's genre is **12 bar blues**.

Koko is divided into an Introduction, seven sections called choruses, and a coda. In jazz music, a chorus is one full statement of a song's form played through. In this case, each chorus contains the complete 12-bar blues progression. Koko is written in the key of E♭ minor, and all the choruses are in 12-bar blues form. Each chorus features different soloists and instrument combinations.

Listen to a recording of Koko on the internet, preferably a recording by Duke Ellington and his Big Band.

Musique Concréte

Musique Concrète was developed in the 1940s by French composer Pierre Schaeffer. It involves composing music based on recorded sounds. Musique concrète uses recordings of natural sounds, like water drips, the human voice, or musical instruments to create aural compositions. The sounds selected and recorded may be modified in various ways. They may be shortened or lengthened, played backwards, or varied in pitch and intensity. The completed work combines all of the sounds into one united composition.

Hugh Le Caine (1914 - 1977)

Hugh Le Caine (1914 -1977) was a Canadian composer and scientist. He received a science degree from Queen's University and worked for the National Research Council of Canada in atomic physics and developing radar systems.

He also focused on electronic music and sound generation and established a studio where he designed electronic instruments. He is considered a pioneer of electronic music.

Dripsody

Dripsody, is an electronic composition, and its genre is **electronic music**. It is an example of musique concrète, and was composed in 1955 by Hugh Le Caine. All of the sounds in this work are derived from the splash of a single drop of water. Le Caine used an eye dropper and recorded the sound of water drops falling into a metal wastebasket for 30 minutes before choosing the sound of one drop on which to base this work. The sound of this drop repeated over and over is heard throughout the work. He manipulated this sound in various ways:

1. He changed the tape speed. Speeding up or slowing down the tape created different pitches. In this way, he was able to assemble some of these pitches into a pentatonic scale.
2. He reversed the tape, playing the sounds backward.
3. He used four different tape loops or recordings of the water to produce repeated patterns or ostinatos.
4. He used tape delay. This was done by playing the sound and re-recording it at the same time creating an echo effect.

The piece begins with a single drop of water and increases in intensity by becoming more rhythmically active and dense until it climaxes in the middle. Then it gradually decreases in intensity and ends where it started, with a single drop of water.

Find a recording of Dripsody on the internet and listen for all of the features listed above.

a) When did the Romantic era occur? _____

b) Music that has a literary or pictorial association is called _____

c) Name two Romantic period composers _____

d) Where was Felix Mendelssohn born? _____

e) Whose music did Mendelssohn help revive? _____

f) What genre is Overture to a Midsummer Nights Dream? _____

g) What author wrote the play that this work is based upon? _____

h) What is the form of Overture to a Midsummer Nights Dream? _____

i) Name the three main sections in this form:

_____   _____   _____

Answer true (T) or false (F) to the following statements.

a. Frédéric Chopin was born in France. _____
b. Chopin composed in the classical era. _____
c. Chopin composed mainly for the piano. _____
d. Chopin wrote in 'bel canto style.' _____
e. 'Nationalism' refers to music with a pictorial or literary association. _____
f. 'Rubato' refers to music from Poland. _____
g. 'Etudes' are sometimes referred to as studies. _____
h. Chopin's Revolutionary Etude is in C minor. _____

Name the composer and genre of the following works:

Petrushka

Composer: _____ Genre: _____

Koko

Composer: _____ Genre: _____

Dripsody

Composer: _____ Genre: _____

Etude Op. 10, No. 12 'Revolutionary'

Composer: _____ Genre: _____

Overture to a Midsummer Nights Dream

Composer: _____ Genre: _____

History Level 8

The Medieval Era (500- 1450)

The medieval era took place from approximately 500 to 1450 A.D. This was a period of heavy church influence. Music was around before this time and had various developments, but during the medieval era, the use and creation of music was regulated by the church.

The church was the main patron of the arts, including music. Many musicians were trained in the church, and the church had the financial means to buy extravagant items like paper, where eventually music was written down. Our current system of music notation is even rooted in the developments made in the medieval church!

Medieval church music had very specific rules, which included the chanting of prayers. Chanting of this period is called **plainchant** and is sometimes referred to as Gregorian chant since Pope Gregory standardized chant for the liturgy. Plainchant is a single line of modal melody, without a measured rhythm, sung in Latin. Modal refers to ancient scales called **modes**, which were studied in Lesson 3.

Plainchant is **monophonic**, meaning it is one melody without harmony, resulting in just one musical part. **Monophony** is a single melody without accompaniment. Monks would sing the prayer together in unison.

Around the year 900, some simple harmony involving two vocal parts was allowed. This type of simple two-part medieval harmony is called **organum**. The harmony was made in one of two ways:

- Sometimes a drone, or low, continuous note, was sung while the main melody was sung at the same time. Drones are still used in bagpipe music today.
- Other times, the words of the song would be sung on two different pitches at the same time.

Ordo Virtutum - Hildegard von Bingen

One of the greatest composers of the medieval era was ***Hildegard von Bingen***. Hildegard lived from approximately 1098 to 1179. She was a German nun, mystic, poet, and composer who was known for her visions and prophecies. Hildegard wrote poems about her visions and prophecies and set them to music.

Her music is incredibly melodic for the middle ages. The church had very stringent rules about music, yet she was able to incorporate new and extended musical techniques that still fit under the guidelines of the church. She used a wide range of pitches and leaps that were uncharacteristic for the time. These methods were used to give meaning and musical emphasis to the words she wrote.

Hildegard's most renowned work is a musical play called ***Ordo Virtutum***. Ordo Virtutum (The Play of the Virtues), composed about 1151, is a liturgical drama, known as a ***morality play***. A morality play is a drama designed to teach a moral or lesson. Ordo Virtutum is about the struggle for a human soul between the Virtues and the Devil. The text of this work is in Latin, the language of the Roman Empire, and the official language of the church.

Ordo Virtutum contains 82 different monophonic melodies. All parts are sung in plainchant by women, except that of the Devil. Several notes are sung to each syllable of text. A technique called ***melisma***, which consists of many notes sung to one syllable, is used to emphasize important words. Hildegard based the music on modes, which serve to elicit varied feelings, like withdrawal, happiness, sadness, or serenity. The rhythm is free, with no time signatures or meter. The characters in Ordo Virtutum are:

- The Soul, Anima, sung by a female voice.
- The Virtues (Humility, Hope, Chastity, Innocence, Contempt of the World, Celestial Love, Discipline, Modesty, Mercy, Victory, Discretion, Patience, Knowledge of God, Charity, Fear of God, Obedience, and Faith), sung by 17 solo female voices.
- The chorus of the Prophets and Patriarchs, sung by women.
- The chorus of Souls, sung by women.
- The Devil (a male voice) does not sing, he only yells or grunts. According to Hildegard, the Devil cannot produce divine harmony.

Secular Music in the Medieval Era

By the late medieval era, **secular**, or non-religious music, was becoming extremely popular. Secular music employed some of the developments that were made within the church. Royalty also played a prominent part in musical life, since wealthy people could afford to train musicians and pay composers to write for them.

Minstrels and **troubadours** were two types of musicians that were part of Royal court life. Minstrels were not as refined as troubadours and entertained in other ways, like juggling. Troubadours sang songs of chivalry, courtly love, and travel to faraway lands. Secular songs developed more and more during this period using multiple voices and instruments.

Sumer is Icumen In

Sumer Is Icumen In is a medieval English vocal work composed in the mid-13th century. This piece is a **rota**. Rota is another word for a round or canon. A round consists of at least two voices that sing the same melody with each voice beginning at different times.

The text of Sumer Is Icumen In is in Middle English, and the title translates to 'Summer is Coming.' The composer is unknown. This is a **polyphonic** composition for six voices. **Polyphony** consists of two or more melodies singing together. In this case, it's six!

Sumer Is Icumen In contains a repeated two-part section called a **pes** (foot). A pes is a melodic or rhythmic pattern that repeats over and over. A pes is also known as an **ostinato**. Below is the four measure pes or ostinato written in modern notation. It is usually sung by two tenors.

The complete melody of Sumer Is Icumen In is shown below. Rather than being written in one of the modes, which was common in the middle ages, it is in a major key. In modern notation you may see it written in 6/8 or 12/8 time and in any number of keys. This example is in F major. Find a recording of this piece on the internet.

The Renaissance Era (ca 1450 - 1600)

The Renaissance Era (ca. 1450-1600) brought about great change in both sacred and secular music. For most of the Medieval Era, music was reserved for the Church and the wealthy. Advancements and social changes in the Renaissance Era allowed music to flourish in both sacred and secular genres. Despite the Reformation and the Counter Reformation, there was continuous musical growth happening in both the Catholic and the Protestant Churches.

In the Renaissance, the motet and the Mass were the most common forms of sacred music. However, many forms of secular music were being developed. Secular music included **madrigals**, which were part songs for several voices, and the rise of both instrumental and dance music.

Josquin Des Prez (ca 1440 - 1521)

Josquin des Prez, from the Renaissance era, became known as one of the greatest composers of the 16th century. He is often just called Josquin. Josquin's date and place of birth are not known, but he was probably born between 1440 and 1450 in France or Belgium. As an adult, he enjoyed a successful musical career in Italy.

Josquin's specialties included the use of overlapping vocals, as found in the canon or round, which is a composition of overlapping vocals in the strictest sense. Using these techniques allowed Josquin to be extremely expressive in the setting of text, while also enriching its meaning. Josquin Des Prez is regarded as one of the leading composers of Renaissance choral music. His compositions are still performed throughout the world today.

El Grillo

"*El Grillo*," or "The Cricket," is a light, fun, *a cappella* piece by Josquin. A cappella refers to vocal music without instrumental accompaniment. El Grillo is considered a *frottola*. This is a polyphonic vocal work, and an ancestor of the madrigal. Josquin wrote three frottole and El Grillo is his most popular. It is written for four voices. The text is in Italian. The English translation of the lyrics are:

> The cricket is a good singer
> Who can hold a long note
> Of drinking the cricket sings
> The cricket is a good singer
> But he doesn't do what birds do,
> After they've sung a bit,
> They go somewhere else,
> The cricket always stays put
> And when the weather is hottest
> He sings solely for love

Josquin uses *word painting* in this piece. Word painting was common in the Renaissance, as the madrigal became popular. Word painting is when the music matches the meaning of the word. For example, on the line "Who can hold a long note," the word "long" is extended. At one point in the refrain, the voices are meant to mimic the chirp of a cricket.

In portions of El Grillo, Josquin uses *homorhythm*. This is a texture where all parts sing in the same rhythm. This rhythm results in a blocked chordal texture. Homorhythmic texture allows the lyrics to be very clear and easy to understand. The opening measures of El Grillo are shown below.

Global Music - The Javanese Gamelan

In 1899, French composer Claude Debussy, upon hearing a Javanese gamelan orchestra wrote: 'Their conservatory is the rhythm of the sea, the wind among the leaves and the thousand sounds of nature...'. For centuries, Indonesians have developed their gamelan orchestras, making sounds that are other worldly, magical, yet still human all at the same time. Since Debussy, other nations have been fascinated and intrigued by this music, and it has spread throughout the world.

The word '**gamelan**' is derived from the Indonesian word meaning 'hammer.' A gamelan is an Indonesian mallet orchestra native to Bali and Java. The gamelan orchestra is made up of several types of mallet instruments like the **metallophone**, a xylophone-like instrument with metal bars struck by mallets, or keyboard-style instruments struck with mallets or hammers, as well as different drums, flutes, and occasionally stringed instruments or vocalists.

Gamelan instruments are tuned differently than those in Western music. There are two tuning systems that gamelan orchestras use, one which consists of five notes, and one which has seven notes. Many of the same instruments occur in pairs, with each one being tuned slightly differently than the other. When two of the same instruments play a note in unison, the different sound waves vibrate against each other, creating a quality of sound gamelan musicians call *ombak*, or 'shimmering sound.'

Traditional Javanese gamelan music is divided into two parts: a central melody, and a part that embellishes that central melody. Gamelan music is not written down or notated. It is handed down orally (or aurally) from generation to generation.

Search the internet for videos and recordings of Gamelan orchestras.

Indian Music - The Raga

Much of Western music is based on modes, especially the major and minor modes. A **raga** is a mode (scale) found in Indian classical music and used in improvised performances. There are over 300 ragas.

Raga means 'color.' Just as each color in the spectrum is unique, each raga has a unique sound. The sound of each raga is associated with certain emotions, times of day, Hindu deities, and seasons. Ragas often use **microtones**. These are smaller intervals than those found in Western music. The traditional half step may be subdivided into quarter steps or quarter tones.

Indian classical music is improvised, so each performance is different. Despite this, Indian musicians do not play whatever they want. Their improvisations must follow the rules of the raga.

Each raga contains:

- the raga scale, which contains the specific pitches used in the piece.
- the Arohana, an ascending form of the scale.
- the Avarohana, a descending form of the scale, which may not be the same as the Arohana.
- the Vadi, an important note that is played more frequently than other notes.
- the Samvadi, a note of seconday importance.

All of these elements work together to form a larger melody called the **chalan**. When musicians master the chalan, they use it as a basis for their improvisation.

The number of instruments in a raga may vary, but there are at least three instruments involved in a performance: a drone, a drummer, and one or more melody instruments. The melody instrument plays the raga. One of the most common Indian melody instruments is the **sitar**, a long-necked, guitar-like, string instrument with a gourd-shaped resonance chamber.

The main percussion instruments used in North India are called **tabla**, a pair of drums that are tuned to work with the notes of the raga. The drums often introduce a regular rhythmic cycle called a **tala**. Tala means 'clap' and is a rhythmic beat that keeps the time of the raga.

The drone instrument is often a **tanpura**. The tanpura looks like a sitar, but has only four strings and is missing the gourd-like resonance chamber. These strings are tuned to the first and fifth scale notes and are played continuously to act as a reference point for the person playing the melody. This helps the soloist stay on track throughout their improvisation.

Find and listen to examples of Indian Raga music on the internet.

Sitar

Tabla

Tanpura

18

Music Analysis

🎵 The Primary Triads

The three most important triads in any key are built on the tonic (I, i), subdominant (IV, iv) and dominant (V). These are known as ***primary triads***. Most folk music, sacred music, all of the blues, and a lot of rock are based on primary triads.

Figure 18.1 contains the well-known hymn "Amazing Grace." The entire hymn is based on I - IV and V.

Figure 18.1

Primary Triad Functions

The Tonic (I or i)

The tonic triad in root position is the strongest chord in tonal music. It is important as a point of departure. Most music begins with the tonic and departs to other chords from it. The tonic might even be more important as a point of arrival. Almost all compositions end on the tonic chord. It acts like the home base for a piece of music. Like gravity, other chords pull towards the tonic.

The Dominant (V)

Some may argue that the dominant chord is the most important chord because of its pull to the tonic. The dominant actually helps us locate the tonic. The presence of the leading tone in the dominant chord creates an anticipation of the tonic chord. The leading tone has a natural tendency to pull to the tonic. Certain chords that contain the leading tone are referred to as **dominant function chords**. V is called the **dominant** because it is the most active dominant function chord.

The Subdominant (IV or iv)

The subdominant chord often leads to the dominant. For this reason, it can be called a **pre-dominant chord**. A pre-dominant chord is a chord that comes before a dominant functioning chord. Movement from chord to chord is called a **harmonic progression**. Movement from the pre-dominant to the dominant to the tonic is one of the strongest progressions in tonal music (IV - V - I).

1. Identify the following chords by writing the functional (Roman numeral) chord symbols under each. (I, IV and V or i, iv and V)

E minor

B minor

F major

A minor

D minor

E major

G flat major

G sharp minor

2. Name the numbered chords as tonic, subdominant or dominant.

Wolfgang Amadeus Mozart

E flat major

1. _____

2. _____

3. _____

4. _____

Harmonic Progression

A ***harmonic progression*** is a succession of two or more chords. In tonal music, a progression is not just any two or more chords. Some progressions are better than others.

The most basic progression in tonal music is I - V - I. We call this the ***fundamental progression***. All that is needed to determine the key of the piece are the V and I (or i) chords. In tonal music, the relationship between the tonic and dominant define the key.

The first phrase of the Sonatina in Figure 18.2 consists of the progression I - V - I - V in D major. This phrase ends on a half cadence (I - V).

The non-chords tones are ***double passing tones***. These passing tones are written in 3rds. Double passing tones are usually written in intervals of 3rds or 6ths.

Figure 18.2

1. Write the functional chord symbol under each chord marked with ★.

7. Answer the questions about the following musical excerpts.
8.

Felix Mendelssohn
(1809 - 1847)

1. Who composed this music? _____

2. Name another composition by this composer. _____

3. In what musical era was it composed? _____

4. How many measures are in this piece? _____

5. Name the key of this piece. _____

6. Add the time signature on the score.

7. Add root/quality chord symbols at the chords marked ★.

8. Name the Intervals at A: _____   B: _____   C: _____   D: _____

9. Define: ***Allegro assai.*** _____

10. Define: ***sfz.*** _____

11. The cadence at E is: ❏ imperfect authentic   ❏ half   ❏ perfect authentic

12. Why are there only 2 beats in the final measure? _____

©San Marco Publications 2023

1. In what musical era was this composed? _____

2. What is the key of this piece? _____

3. Write the time signature on the score.

4. Name the chord at A: _____

5. In this key, the chord at A is the: ☐tonic chord   ☐subdominant chord   ☐dominant chord

6. Name the chord at B: _____

7. In this key, B is the: ☐tonic chord   ☐subdominant chord   ☐dominant chord

8. Name the non-chord tones at C: _____ D: _____

9. Define *Allegretto*: _____

10. Define *fp*: _____

11. Does the melody end on a stable or unstable chord tone? _____

George Frideric Handel
(1685 - 1759)

1. Name the composer of this piece. _____

2. Name another composition by this composer. _____

3. What musical period was this piece composed? _____

4. Name the key of this piece. _____

5. Write the time signature on the score.

6. This is an example of: ❏simple triple time   ❏compound triple time

7. The chord at A is the: ❏tonic chord   ❏subdominant chord   ❏dominant chord

8. The chord at B is the: ❏tonic chord   ❏subdominant chord   ❏dominant chord

9. The chord at C is the: ❏tonic chord   ❏subdominant chord   ❏dominant chord

10. How many times does the tonic chord appear in this excerpt? _____

11. Name the intervals at D: _____   E: _____   F: _____

12. How many times does the leading tone appear in this piece? _____

13. How many times does the subtonic appear in this piece? _____

©San Marco Publications 2023   Music Analysis

1. Name the key of this piece. _____

2. Write the time signature directly on the score.

3. This piece is written for a melody with piano accompaniment. This is and example of:

    ❏ polyphonic texture ❏ homophonic texture ❏ counterpoint ❏ monophonic texture

4. In what musical era was this piece composed? _____

5. Name another composer from the same era. _____

6. Add the correct rest or rests to the voice part in m.1.

7. Name the interval at A: _____

8. Name the interval at B: _____

9. Name the interval at C: _____

10. Find and circle one leading tone in the voice part. Label it LT.

❽ 1. For the given musical excerpt, answer the questions that follow.

Sensucht nach dem Fruhling

Wolfgang Amadeus Mozart
(1756- 1791)

a. Name the key of this piece. _____

b. Write the time signature directly on the score.

c. In what musical period was this piece composed? _____

d. Mark the phrases directly on the score.

e. Is this an example of a: ❑ parallel period ❑ contrasting period

f. Mark the form on the score using the letters **a**, **a¹**, or **b**.

g. State the implied harmony using functional and root/quality chord symbols.

h. Circle and identify any non-chord tones.

❽ 2. For the given musical excerpt, answer the questions that follow.

Sonatina
III

Matthew Camidge
(1758- 1844)

cadence:_____

cadence:_____

a. Name the key of this piece. _____

b. Write the time signature directly on the score.

c. In what musical period was this piece composed? _____

d. Mark the phrases directly on the score.

e. Is this an example of a: ❑parallel period   ❑contrasting period

f. Mark the form on the score using the letters **a**, **a¹**, or **b**.

g. State the implied harmony using functional and root/quality chord symbols.

h. Circle and identify any non-chord tones.

i. Write the name of the cadences at the end of each phrase in the place provided on the score.

Voice Leading

Voice leading is concerned with the horizontal or linear aspect of music and is as important as the vertical or chordal aspect. Voice leading is very important in polyphonic music since it consists of the performance of more than one melody at the same time. Examples of this can be found in the Two-Part Inventions of J.S. Bach.

There are four types of motion that can occur between two voices horizontally.

1. ***Contrary motion*** occurs when two voices move in the opposite direction. Figure 18.3 shows voices moving in contrary motion.

Figure 18.3

2. ***Oblique motion*** occurs when one voice is stationary, while the second voice moves to another pitch (up or down). Figure 18.4 shows voices moving in oblique motion.

Figure 18.4

3. ***Similar motion*** occurs when two voices move in the same direction (up or down), but not by the same interval. Figure 18.5 shows voices moving in similar motion.

Figure 18.5

4. ***Parallel motion*** occurs when two voices move in the same direction (up or down), by the same basic interval. Figure 18.6 shows voices moving in parallel motion.

Figure 18.6

5. ***Static motion*** occurs when two voices hold their notes and repeat. Actually there is no motion happening at all, only repetition. Figure 18.7 shows voices in static motion.

Figure 18.7

❽ 1. List the type of motion in each example. Contrary, oblique, similar, or parallel.

Study the voice leading in Figure 18.8. Both (a) and (b) are examples of parallel motion. However, there is a difference. The intervals in (a) are a major 6th and a minor 6th, while the intervals in (b) are both major 6ths. The term parallel motion does not always mean the intervals are exactly the same. The *number* is the same, but the *quality* can be different. Both intervals move in parallel motion but technically (b) is more parallel than (a). The term parallel motion does not take into account the quality of the interval.

Figure 18.8

In traditional harmony and counterpoint, certain parallel perfect intervals are forbidden. These intervals are parallel perfect 5ths, parallel perfect octaves, and parallel perfect unisons. These intervals are very consonant, and when they move in parallel motion, they can lose their individual identity. The first three examples of parallel motion in Figure 18.9 should be avoided. However, a diminished 5th followed by a perfect 5th is fine.

Figure 18.9

❽ 1. The following voices move in parallel motion. Mark the correct examples with ✓ and the incorrect examples with ✗.

2. Answer the questions that deal with the following musical examples.

Franz Joseph Haydn
Op.74, No. 3

a. Name the key of this phrase. _____

b. Write the time signature directly on the score.

c. In what musical period was this piece composed? _____

d. What open score is this written for? _____

e. State the implied harmony using functional and root/quality chord symbols on the score.

f. Find and circle a melodic sequence.

g. Name the cadence at the end of this phrase. _____

Passepied

George Frideric Handel
(1685-1759)

a. Add the correct time signature directly on the music.

b. Name the key of this piece._____

c. Name the composer of this piece. _____

d. Name another composition by this composer. _____

d. In what musical era was this composed? _____

e. This piece is: ❑ monophonic   ❑ polyphonic

f. Identify the motion at:

A:	❑ contrary	❑ parallel	❑ similar	❑ oblique
B:	❑ contrary	❑ parallel	❑ similar	❑ oblique
C:	❑ contrary	❑ parallel	❑ similar	❑ oblique
D:	❑ contrary	❑ parallel	❑ similar	❑ oblique
E:	❑ contrary	❑ parallel	❑ similar	❑ oblique
F:	❑ contrary	❑ parallel	❑ similar	❑ oblique

Music Terms and Signs

Terms

accelerando, accel.	becoming quicker
accent	a stressed note
ad libitum, ad lib.	at the liberty of the performer
adagio	slow
agitato	agitated
alla, all'	in the manner of
allargando	getting slower and broader
allegretto	fairly fast, a little slower than allegro
allegro	fast
andante	moderately slow, at a walking pace
andantino	a little faster than andante
animato	lively, animated
arco	for strings return to bowing after pizzicato or col legno.
attacca	begin immediately, proceed without a break
a tempo	return to the original tempo
ben, bene	well
bewegt	with movement, agitated
calando	becoming slower and softer
cantabile	in a singing style
cédez	yield, slow down
col, coll', colla, colle	with
comodo	at a comfortable tempo
con	with
con brio	with vigor
con espressione	with expression
con fuoco	with fire
con grazia	with grace
con moto	with motion
con sordino	with the use of a mute

crescendo, cresc.	becoming louder
da capo, D.C.	from the beginning
D.C. al fine	repeat from the beginning and end at *Fine*
dal segno, D.S. 𝄋	from the sign
decrescendo, decresc.	becoming softer
diminuendo, dim.	becoming softer
dolce	sweetly, gentle
dolente	sad
e, ed	and
espressivio, espress.	expressive, with expression
fine	the end
forte, f	loud
fortissimo, ff	very loud
fortepiano, fp	loud, then suddenly soft
giocoso	humorous, joyful
grandioso	grand, play in a grand and noble style
grazioso	gracefully
grave	slow and solemn
langsam	slowly
largamente	broadly
larghetto	fairly slow, not as slow as largo
largo	very slow
léger	lightly
leggiero	light
lentement	slowly
lento	slow
l'istesso tempo	at the same tempo
loco	return to the normal register
ma	but
maestoso	majestically
mano destra, m.d.	right hand

mano sinistra, m.s.	left hand
marcato	play marked or stressed
martellato	strongly accented, hammered
mässig	moderately
meno	less
meno mosso	less motion
mesto	sad, mournful
mezzo forte, mf	moderately loud
mezzo piano, mp	moderately soft
mit Ausdruck	with expression
moderato	at a moderate tempo
modéré	at a moderate tempo
molto	much, very
morendo	dying, fading away
mouvement	movement, tempo, motion
non	not
ottava, 8va	the interval of an octave
pesante	heavy, play with weight
pedale, ped	pedal
pianissimo, pp	very soft
piano, p	soft
piu	more
piu mosso	more motion
pizzicato	pluck the strings, for string instruments
poco	little
poco a poco	little by little
prestissimo	as fast as possible
presto	very fast
primo, prima	first, the upper part of a duet
quasi	almost, as if
quindicesima alta, 15ma	play 2 octaves higher

rallentando, rall.	slowing down
risoluto	resolute, bold, strong
ritardando, rit.	slowing down gradually
ritenuto, riten	suddenly slower
rubato	flexible tempo with slight variations of speed to enhance musical expression.
scherzando	playful, play in a light-hearted happy manner
schnell	fast
sehr	very
secondo, seconda	second, lower part of a duet
semplice	simple
sempre	always
senza	without
sforzando, sf, sfz	sudden strong accent on a single note or chord
simile	continue in the same manner as has just been indicated
sonore	sonorous, resonant; with rich tone
sopra	above, indicates piano player crossing hands
sostentuto	sustained, play in a prolonged manner
staccato	play short and detached
stringendo	gradually faster, pressing forward
subito	suddenly
tacet	be silent, voice or instrument does not play or sing
tempo	speed at which music is performed
Tempo Primo, Tempo I	return to the original tempo
tranquillo	tranquil, quiet
tre corde	3 strings, release the left pedal on the piano
troppo	too much
tutti	a passage for the whole ensemble
una corda	1 string, depress the left pedal on the piano
vite	fast

vivace   lively, brisk

vivo   lively

volta   time, *prima volta*=1st time, *seconda volta*=2nd time

volti subito, v.s.   turn the page quickly

Signs

accent - a stressed note

common time - symbol for 4/4

crescendo - becoming louder

decrescendo - becoming softer

double bar line - the end of a piece

fermata - hold note or rest longer than written value

glissando, gliss - a continuous sliding up or down from one pitch to another

slur - play the notes smoothly (legato)

staccato - play short and detached

tie - hold for the combined value of the tied notes

repeat marks - at the second sign go back to the first sign and repeat the music from there. The first sign is left out if the music is repeated from the beginning.

pedal symbol - press/release the right pedal.

tenuto mark - when placed over or under a note, hold it for its full value.

dal segno, D.S. - from the sign.

8va - play one octave higher than written pitch.

8va - play one octave lower than written pitch.

down bow - on a string instrument, play the note by drawing the bow downward.

up bow - on a string instrument, play the note by drawing the bow upward.

breath mark - take a breath or a small break

Terms and Signs

Exam Level 7

1. Identify the following scales as: major, natural minor, harmonic minor, melodic minor, chromatic, whole tone, octatonic, major pentatonic, minor pentatonic, or blues.

Scale: _____

Scale: _____

Scale: _____

Scale: _____

Scale: _____

2. Add rests under the brackets to complete each measure.

3. Write the following intervals above the given notes. Invert them and rename them.

4. For the following antecedent phrase: a) Name the key. b) Compose a consequent phrase creating a contrasting period. c) Write a cadence in keyboard style at the end of each phrase. d) Name the cadences you have written.

5. Name the key of the following melody. Transpose it down a perfect 5th. Name the new key.

___ 6. Write the following chords using the correct key signature for each.
10

The supertonic triad of E♭ major in 1st inversion

The mediant triad of F♯ major in root position.

The leading note triad of G minor in 2nd inversion

The dominant triad of C♯ minor in 1st inversion

The submediant triad of A major in root position

vii°⁷ of F minor

V⁷ of D minor

vii°⁷ of B minor

V⁷ of A minor

V⁷ of B major

___ 7. Match the following Italian terms with their meanings.
10

____ *morendo*   a) playful

____ *semplice*   b) sad

____ *scherzando*   c) simple

____ *pesante*   d) dying away

____ *mesto*   e) heavy, with emphasis

___ 8. For the following cadences, name the key, identify them as perfect authentic, imperfect authentic or half. Add functional chord symbols to each cadence.
10

Key:_____   Key:_____

Cadence:_____   Cadence:_____

Key:_____   Cadence:_____   Key:_____   Cadence:_____

9. Answer questions dealing with the following musical excerpt.

Tobias Haslinger
Sonatina in C major, II

a) Name the key of this piece _____

b) Write the time signature on the score.

c) Name the chord at A: root _____ quality _____ inversion _____

d) Name the chord at B: root _____ quality _____ inversion _____

e) Name the chord at C: root _____ quality _____ inversion _____

f) Name the chord at D: root _____ quality _____ inversion _____

g) Give the function of the non-chord tones at E: _____ F: _____

h) Name the interval at G: _____

i) Give the term for the notes at H: _____

j) Define: *giocoso*: _____

j) The cadence at I is: ❏ perfect authentic   ❏ half   ❏ imperfect authentic

10. Name the composer and musical period for the following compositions.

Composition	Composer	Musical Era
Dripsody		
Revolutionary Etude		
Koko		
Overture to a Midsummer Nights Dream		
Petrushka		

Exam Level 8

1. Write the following scales and modes ascending and descending.

F chromatic scale

C blues scale

G♭ major scale

D octatonic scale

C lydian mode

E♭ dorian mode

A locrian mode

B mixolydian mode

___ 5. Name the following chords as: tone cluster, polychord, quartal chord, diminished 7th, dominant 7th, major triad, minor triad, augmented triad or diminished triad.
10

___ 6. For the following melodic fragment:
10
- Name the key.
- Complete the consequent (a) phrase, ending on an unstable scale degree.
- Write an antecedent (b) phrase creating a conrasting period.
- Name each cadence.

Key: _____

___ 7. Add rests to complete the following measure.
10

___ 8. Transcribe the following passsage into short score
10

Giovanni Croce
Is it Nothing to You?

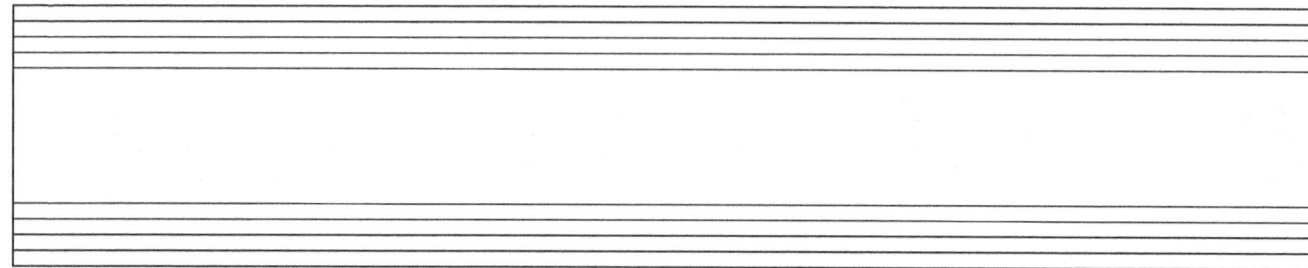

9. Give the best answer to the following statements:

a. an Italian term that means 'suddenly slower.' _____
b. an Indonesian mallet orchestra native to Bali and Java. _____
c. an Italian term that means 'with mute.' _____
d. a mode found in Indian classical music and used in improvised performances. _____
e. the composer of 'El Grillo.' _____
f. a German term meaning 'fast.' _____
g. a single melody without accompaniment. _____
h. a texture where there all parts sing in the same rhythm. _____
i. a French term meaning 'lightly.' _____
j. name for musical era between ca.1450 - 1600. _____
k. the composer of 'Ordo Virtutum.' _____
l. two or more independant melodies singing together. _____
m. a long-necked, guitar-like, string instrument with a gourd shaped resonance chamber used in Indian music. _____
n. a polyphonic vocal work and an ancestor of the madrigal. _____
o. a German term meaning 'slowly.' _____
p. vocal music without instrumental accompaniment. _____
q. a melodic or rhythmic pattern that repeats over and over. _____
r. name for musical era between ca. 500 - 1450. _____
s. means 'clap' and is a rhythmic beat that keeps the time of a raga. _____
t. a single line of modal melody, without a measured rhythm, sung in Latin. _____

10. Answer questions dealing with the following musical excerpt.

Ludwig van Beethoven
String Quartet No.16

a) Name the key of this piece _____

b) Name the enharmonic tonic minor for this key._____

c) Write the time signature directly on the score.

d) Check two words that describe this time signature:

❑simple   ❑duple   ❑compound   ❑triple   ❑quadruple

e) Name the intervals at A: _____ B:_____ C:_____

f) Define **Lento assai**: _____

g) How are mm.7, 8, and 9 related? _____
_____

h) This is an excerpt from a string quartet. What instument is it written for?_____

i) Name the four instruments of the string quartet.

_____ _____ _____ _____

©San Marco Publications 2023   Exam

www.ingramcontent.com/pod-product-compliance
Lightning Source LLC
Chambersburg PA
CBHW081616100526
44590CB00021B/3461